PSYCHOLINGUISTICS

PSYCHOLINGUISTICS

DAN I. SLOBIN

University of California, Berkeley

Scott, Foresman and Company
Glenview, Illinois   London

To my parents,
Norval and Judith Slobin

Foreword

Both the content and the format of the beginning course in psychology vary widely today, not only between institutions and departments but also between instructors within the same department. There is a range of acceptable possibilities for organizing the course and considerable freedom for the instructor to select and emphasize those aspects of modern psychology which he considers most important and useful. One of the major reasons for course differences is the variety of subject matter and topics that are grouped under psychology. It is impossible to give adequate treatment to all the relevant topics within the time limitations typically imposed on the introductory course. To make matters more complicated, the accumulation of knowledge is proceeding at such a rapid pace in the different areas of psychology that it is virtually impossible for anyone to keep pace with new developments in all these fields. Thus, an instructor often rightfully limits his treatment to those topics which he feels competent to present with knowledge and understanding. Finally, the current emphasis, in response largely to student and public demand, on the uses of psychology, on its relevance, must be noted. To be sure, not all instructors are convinced of the appropriateness of teaching the application of psychology in the beginning course, pointing to the potential dangers of a little knowledge and of premature attempts to use information not well-tested or standardized. In contrast, however, many who teach the introductory course give considerable time and attention to the application and the meaning of what is known.

With this variety in content, technique, and orientation among instructors, there is need for a corresponding variety of textual material. The Scott, Foresman Basic Psychological Concepts Series has been prepared in response to that need. Each title within the Series addresses a single topic. While the volumes are relatively brief, each gives a more intensified development of the topic than is available in any omnibus introductory textbook. Each volume has been prepared by an expert, who presents not only full knowledge of the current substantive and methodological state of his field, but who also provides an original and creative treatment of this material. The books are more than the typical cut-and-dried survey of a topic. There is room in each for the kind of original analysis of the problem heretofore unavailable in introductory reading.

Each title in the Series is independent of the others. They all have been written as a whole so as to maximize the coverage of psychology with minimal overlap and redundancy. No single title is a prerequisite to any other in the Series. At the same time, however, the initial volume, an *Introduction to Psychology*, sets the tone for the Series and attempts to explain how various topics are interrelated. In addition, we should note that there is considerable cross-referencing among the volumes and a general attempt at integrating facts and theories that are pertinent to several topics. While the titles are independent and may be used alone, they are also part of a larger, coordinated, comprehensive survey and interpretation of psychology.

The purpose of the Series is to provide both flexibility and expertise for the instructor and the student in the beginning course. The Series is adaptable to a variety of educational goals. The teacher can select and construct a set of reading units, with the content, emphasis, and sequence he desires and that will fit the general purpose and orientation of this course. He may, for example, base his course on several selected topics, each of which is developed in a separate volume. Alternatively, he might use only a single volume to fill a void or to further develop a topic of special importance. Volumes from the Series may be used in conjunction with most general textbooks or with the initial core book in the Series. It is furthermore conceivable that one or another of the volumes would be useful in advanced courses, as preliminary reading for the student ill-prepared to contend with a topic on that level or as a supplement developing the background in a related topic. Because of the distinguished authorship of this Series, the teacher can feel confident in his selection without fear of uneven quality, superficiality, or duplication. This Series has a variety of uses at different educational levels, depending upon the needs of the student, the purpose of the course, and the creativity and imagination of the instructor.

The present volume, *Psycholinguistics*, by Dan I. Slobin, deals with a topic not typically treated in depth in current textual materials for the introductory course. No one is likely to quarrel with the statement that language plays an intimate and vital, if complex, role in human behavior. Still, for some reason—perhaps because of the very obviousness of the process or, more probably, because of its complexity—psychologists have been slow to study and consequently to make progress toward an understanding of language until rather recently. In the last ten years or so, however, the intriguing problems of psycholinguistics have attracted the attention and imagination of many young researchers and theorists. Our understanding of linguistic behavior has begun to develop, and we are now at a point in the science where it becomes reasonable to speak of the principles of psycholinguistics. Professor Slobin's volume presents and interprets these principles.

We believe that students will find the material fascinating and challenging. We believe further that instructors who might formerly have skimmed the area of linguistic behavior in their lectures for lack of adequate textual material will find it possible to treat this topic comprehensively with *Psycholinguistics* as a resource for their students.

Lyle E. Bourne, Jr., Series Editor, University of Colorado
Leonard Berkowitz, Series Editor, University of Wisconsin

Preface

The purpose of this book is to acquaint the nonspecialist with some of the methods and implications of the psychological study of language and speech. The implications of the young and burgeoning field of psycholinguistics bear upon persistent and ancient problems of philosophy and psychology—problems of the nature and development of the human mind. This book, being brief and introductory, can only highlight some of the major issues which have excited psycholinguists during the past decade. And, indeed, the rapid growth of the field embraces little more than a decade. The publication in 1957 of Noam Chomsky's revolutionary little book, *Syntactic Structures*, heralded the beginning of the challenges posed to traditional linguistics and psychology by transformational grammar. In the early 1960's George Miller and his students at Harvard's Center for Cognitive Studies began to probe transformational grammar in the context of the psychological laboratory. At the same time, language development in the child became the focus of psycholinguistic investigation in the pioneering studies of Roger Brown and his colleagues at Harvard, Susan Ervin-Tripp and Wick Miller at Berkeley, and Martin Braine at Walter Reed in Maryland. Eric Lenneberg, also at Harvard, was exploring the biological foundations of human language. Now, training and research in psycholinguistics can be found in the major universities of North America, western and eastern Europe, the Soviet Union, and Japan.

Given the current extent and diversity of the field, I am certain that various of my colleagues will find this little book deficient in its reflection of one or another aspect of psycholinguistics. Rather than apologize in advance, however, let me express the hope that the reader will be sufficiently engaged by the questions raised here to go on and fill in those gaps on his own. Many references to related materials are provided for that purpose.

This book has grown out of an undergraduate course in psycholinguistics which I have been teaching at Berkeley for the past five years. Rather than present an entire twenty-week course here, I have selected some topics for emphasis. Topics especially slighted here include phonology and speech perception, biological foundations of language, animal communication, and the new field of sociolinguistics. In condensing part of the course to cold type, I have attempted to retain some of the more direct and personal style of lecturing. From time to time I have felt free to quote from the writings of distinguished colleagues, living and dead, in order to somewhat enrich my monologue. I owe much of the style and content of this book to the many students who helped me learn about psycholinguistics as I tried to help them learn.

First of all, then, I must thank my students—for their questioning, for their misunderstanding and understanding, and for their appreciation of psycholinguistics. And then I must thank my own teachers—Roger Brown, Jerome Bruner, Eric Lenneberg, and George Miller—who got me started on the particular constellation of interests reflected here. Many good colleagues, at Berkeley and elsewhere, have left their marks as well; I am sure they will be able to find signs of their influences here. And I must thank my wife Kathy whose meticulous reading of the first draft prevented much unclear and awkward writing from appearing in print. As is customary, of course, I accept responsibility for the form in which I have conveyed the ideas of my teachers and colleagues.

Dan I. Slobin
Berkeley, California
May 1969

Table of Contents

Introduction

Psycholinguistics brings together the theoretical and empirical tools of both psychology and linguistics to study the mental processes underlying the acquisition and use of language. The field is thus truly interdisciplinary. Linguists are engaged in the formal description of an important segment of human knowledge—namely the structure of language. This structure includes speech sounds and meanings, and the complex system of grammar, which relates sounds and meanings. Psychologists want to know how children acquire such systems and how such systems function when people are actually speaking and understanding sentences.

In brief, then, psycholinguists are interested in the underlying knowledge and abilities which people must have in order to use language and in order to learn to use language in childhood. I say "*underlying* knowledge and abilities" because language, like all systems of human knowledge, can only be inferred from the careful study of overt behavior. We are concerned here with the overt behavior of speaking and understanding speech. Thus, the problem of the psycholinguist is that of all social scientists who venture beyond description of behavior—namely, to postulate underlying structures and processes which may account for apparent orderliness in observed behavior.

It is important to grasp the distinction between overt behavior and underlying structure. In English, and other languages, the distinction is expressed in the concepts of *language* and *speech: speech* has a corresponding verb form, whereas *language* does not. We say: "He speaks the English language." To speak is to produce meaningful sounds. These sounds have meaning because they are systematically related to something called "the English language." Speech is behavior. You can listen to it; you can record it on magnetic tape. You cannot tape record the English language. You can only record English speech. Because we know the English language, we can understand each other's speech. Language is thus something we *know*. The English language is a body of knowledge represented in the brains of speakers of English. The description of such bodies of knowledge has been traditionally the province of linguistics, while psychology has traditionally defined itself as "the science of human behavior." It should become clear to you, however, that this border between disciplines cannot reasonably be drawn. We cannot study behavior without a theory of the structure of that behavior, and we cannot study the structure without being concerned with the behavior in which the structure is manifested. In fact, Noam Chomsky, whose pioneering work in transformational grammar has revolutionized modern linguistics, defines the potential contributions of his field in terms of characterization of cognitive systems and general properties of human intelligence. "Linguistics, so characterized," he says, "is simply the subfield of psychology that deals with these aspects of mind" (1968, p. 24).

Psychology itself, of course, has long been concerned with the contents of the "black box," and there is a vast literature dealing with a multifarious array of "intervening variables" and "hypothetical constructs" in psychology. Even the performance of rats in mazes has been exhaustively debated in terms of "learning" and "performance," as psychologists argued about the distinction between what the rat actually did in the maze and what he may have learned about the maze. We will encounter a similar distinction in psycholinguistic discussions of "competence" and "performance"—a distinction between what an individual is theoretically *competent* of speaking and understanding and what he actually *does* speak and understand in given situations.

The special appeal of linguistics to psychologists lies in the fact that linguists have provided us with one of the most detailed and provocative available descriptions of a segment of human knowledge. In the past decade or so, psychologists have been especially stimulated by the revolutionary approaches to linguistics developed by Noam Chomsky and his colleagues at Massachusetts Institute of Technology. It is especially in the field of grammar that modern linguistics has had a significant impact on psychology. This work has enriched theory and research in the psychology of cognition, and serves as the most fitting beginning for an exploration of psycholinguistics.

1

Grammar and Psychology

I have tried to suggest that the study of language may very well, as was traditionally supposed, provide a remarkably favorable perspective for the study of human mental processes.

—Noam Chomsky (1968, p. 84)

The study of grammar is something most people try to avoid after years of traumatic encounters with it in "grammar school" and in later schooling. Why should a psychologist care about such a dry and formalistic field? The sort of grammar which makes people shudder is *prescriptive* grammar—the rules of how educated people "ought to" speak and write. But there is another kind of grammar—a *descriptive* grammar which attempts to describe the knowledge which people must have in order to speak and understand language. It is this sort of grammar which has excited psychologists because it promises to tell us something important about the nature of the human mind.

What sort of thing is this grammar? What does grammar do? One way of looking at this question is to take a collection of words and see some of the ways in which they can be arranged. Consider the following three strings of words:

(1) pie little blue mud make eye girl was
(2) the little pie with mud eyes was making a blue girl
(3) the little girl with blue eyes was making a mud pie

People would probably agree that the first string of words is not a sentence; this is one way of saying that it has no grammar. The second and third strings are sentences, though one is extremely anomalous and the other is not. If you read these strings out loud and ask people to remember them, they find (1) hardest to remember and (3) easiest. It is of interest that people can remember the sentences better than the unstructured string (1), even though the sentences have more words and parts of words (suffixes) than the unstructured string. What has been added to the collection of words to make it a grammatical entity?

The most obvious addition in strings (2) and (3), in comparison with (1), is order. Not only does order make the whole sequence more coherent, but it also gives other information: Order (in English) tells us about the subject-object relationship. For example, in (3) the sequence of *girl* —*making*—*mud pie* establishes who is doing what to what.

There is also the addition of "markers." There are two types of markers here: *function words (the, a, with)* and *suffixes (-s, -ing)*. The markers do such things as identify classes (for example, *the* identifies a noun), specify relations (*with* relates *girl* to *eyes*), or signal meanings (-*ing* signals ongoing activity, -*s* signals plurality), and so on.

All of these things together—order and various forms of markers

—make up grammar, and convert a disconnected string of words into a sentence. Grammar lies between the speech sounds you hear or say and the meanings you connect with them. You can only make sense of the strings of words you hear if you "know" (in some unconscious sense) the grammar of your language. You can only communicate with someone else if both of you have the same underlying knowledge of the language.

One part of grammar, called *syntax*, deals with the way in which sentences are put together. The study of syntax brings us face to face with one of the most important aspects of human language: its productivity. We are almost never called upon to create new words, and most of the sentences we hear do not contain new words to be understood; but we are continually being called upon to create and understand new sentences. This fact often comes as a surprise. Somehow it seems intuitively that the stock of sentences could not be so large. To convince yourself that the stock of possible sentences is, for all practical purposes, infinite, just try this exercise: Take any book, read a sentence (say, this very sentence), and then see how far you have to read to find that sentence repeated again. Unless you have chosen a cliché, or a theme which is quoted again and again, I think you will find the job hopeless. Sentences are, by and large, novel events.

A central question of modern linguistics, therefore, is this: How can a new sentence be understood (or produced)? We can learn our vocabularies by rote; we cannot learn our sentences by rote. This impels us to speak of the learning or formation of something which is psychologically equivalent to a system of *rules*, whereby we can extend a limited amount of experience with a limited number of sentences to the capacity to produce and understand an unlimited number of sentences. One of the central problems of psycholinguistics is to understand the nature and development of this capacity.

It should be made clear that the use of the word *rule* does not mean that psycholinguists believe people can state explicit rules of grammar, or that children learn such rules. None of us can state all the rules of English grammar; indeed, all these rules have not yet been explicitly worked out by the most skillful linguists. The crucial (and perplexing) phrase in the paragraph above is "something which is *psychologically equivalent* to a system of rules." As the Berkeley psycholinguist Susan Ervin-Tripp has put it: "To qualify as a native speaker . . . one must learn . . . rules. . . . This is to say, of course, that one must learn to behave *as though one knew the rules*" (my italics) (Slobin, 1967, p. x). The problem of rules is discussed in greater detail in Chapter 3. The central point is that a child has learned much more than a list of specific word combinations. He has acquired knowledge that makes it possible for him to go beyond the specific collection of sentences he has heard, speaking and comprehending an endless variety of new utterances.

Let us look more closely at the kind of underlying knowledge you have of the structure of English, for it is just such knowledge which must be accounted for by syntactic theory.[1] Such a theory will have to account for various things which we language-users know implicitly about our language and various things we can do with our language. English examples are used here simply because we are English-speakers, but the facts presented below undoubtedly hold for all human beings, regardless of the languages they speak. The following sorts of facts represent universal aspects of linguistic competence.

LINGUISTIC INTUITIONS

Grammaticality

You are able to distinguish well-formed sentences from ungrammatical strings. You had no trouble, above, in distinguishing between an unstructured string of words (1), an anomalous sentence (2), and an unanomalous sentence (3). You would also agree that certain word sequences are not grammatical sentences. To take an example from Chomsky (1957, p. 36), we know that (4) and (5) are grammatical sentences of English, but that (6) is not:

(4) The scene of the movie was in Chicago.

(5) The scene that I wrote was in Chicago.

(6) The scene of the movie and that I wrote was in Chicago.

This is one sort of knowledge which a grammar of English must account for.

Note that this example also demonstrates that we know how to put sentences together into longer sentences: (6) is incorrect, but we know that it is correct to put (4) and (5) together in a variety of ways, such as:

(7) The scene of the movie that I wrote was in Chicago.

Your sense of grammaticality also includes some knowledge of degree of deviation of sentences from English. For example, most English-speakers would probably agree in scaling the following three sentences (from Lees, 1957) in terms of "degree of deviation from English":

(8) The dog looks terrifying.

(9) The dog looks barking.

(10) The dog looks lamb.

You are also able to interpret deviant sentences such as (9) or (10). In

---

[1]This book leans heavily upon syntactic theory as developed within the framework of transformational generative grammar (Chomsky, 1957, 1964, 1965; Katz and Postal, 1964). In fairness to the reader, it should be pointed out that this approach, though extremely influential, has not been unanimously or unequivocally embraced by linguists.

fact, much of the understanding of certain kinds of poetry is based on this ability to find interpretations for grammatically unusual constructions — an activity which can be especially pleasurable.

Grammatical Relations

When perceiving a sentence you are able to determine which noun is subject and which is object, what words modify a given noun, the relationship of the nouns to the verbs, and so on. For example, consider a pair of apparently similar sentences, oft-quoted in the linguistic literature:

(11) John is easy to please.

(12) John is eager to please.

Somehow you know that *John* is the object of the first sentence ("Somebody pleases John") and subject of the second ("John pleases somebody"). Although the two sentences appear to have similar structures on the surface, at some deeper level they have quite different meanings. This is a central point of transformational grammar: people are able to go beneath the surface structures of sentences, transforming those structures into deeper structures which reveal underlying meanings.

Sentence Relations

Another ability which a syntactic theory must account for is the fact that you can appreciate relations between sentence types. For example, you know that (13) and (14) mean the same thing:

(13) The President makes the decisions.

(14) The decisions are made by the President.

You know this, in part, because of the ability discussed above — the ability to determine underlying grammatical relations in a sentence. Thus you know that the logical propositions underlying the active (13) and passive (14) sentences above are identical, though the word order is changed. You also know how to turn sentences into questions, how to negate sentences, how to conjoin sentences (as in examples 4 – 7), how to turn sentences into relative clauses, and so on. To repeat the terminology used above, you know that (13) and (14) mean the same thing because, although they have different "surface structures," they have similar "deep structures."

Ambiguity

A theory of syntax must also account for the fact that we can recognize syntactic ambiguity. That is to say, there are some sentences which can have several interpretations. For example, consider the sentence:

(15) Visiting relatives can be a nuisance.

One way in which we can "disambiguate" such a sentence is to relate it to different propositions which, in some sense, may be thought of as underlying sentence (15). We can explain the ambiguity by showing that the sentence can be related to two other sentences, in which the ambiguous *can be* is realized in two different ways:

(16) Visiting relatives are a nuisance.

(17) Visiting relatives is a nuisance.

Again, we can say that there is a difference here between surface and deep structure: This sentence (15) has one surface structure, but two different deep, or underlying, structures.

GRAMMAR AS THEORY

In short, the goal of syntactic theory is to account for linguistic intuitions. It is in this sense that transformationalists assert that *a grammar is a theory of a language*. It is a theory which should be able to discriminate sentences from nonsentences, assign degrees of deviance to nonsentences, relate sentence structures to both meanings and sounds, and it is a theory which should be able to account for, or "generate," all possible sentences of the language. The word "theory" is used here in the sense of any scientific theory. In your childhood you were able to induce the underlying regularities of the language you heard spoken, and this knowledge enables you to produce and to recognize new regularities in the system. One linguist, Lees, has phrased the task in the following terms: "Grammar should be a maximally general set of statements which accounts for not only utterances in the corpus [of speech examined by the linguist], but all possible utterances. . . . Grammar must generate all and only the grammatical sentences of the language" (1957).

A grammar is an attempt to characterize the kind of *knowledge* or *competence* human beings must have in order to use language. The sort of competence in which we are interested can be defined, in part, in terms of the subheadings of the last few pages: the language-user's knowledge of grammaticality, grammatical relations, sentence relations, ambiguity, and so on.

One way to conceptualize the matter is to look at the linguists' interest as an attempt to build a machine which could treat sentences in the manner discussed above. Then you could look at the linguistic rules, which Chomsky and others have written, as rules or instructions which you would give to a machine, and see if the machine could in fact indicate if a sentence was grammatical, or if it was ambiguous. Or you could program the machine to produce sentences according to such rules, and determine if it could produce a full range of sentences, all of which were grammatical. Although it would certainly be interesting, and perhaps practical to build such a machine, the main point of this example is theoretical. If a machine can be programmed to perform in human-like ways, it might be assumed that the rules underlying the machine's performance have some psychological equivalent. Thus the exercise of programming the machine serves to sharpen our notions of the sorts of knowledge people must have in order to demonstrate linguistic intuitions such as those discussed above. The success of a machine program based upon a linguistic rule system would suggest that the knowledge of language reflected in that rule system is, in some sense, "psychologically real."

COMPETENCE AND PERFORMANCE

It would be a great accomplishment to formulate rules which would enable a machine to make the same linguistic judgments as are made by human beings. But note that we are dealing with a very limited sort of performance here, such as rating sentences for grammaticality or producing isolated sentences outside of the context of normal human communication. This limited sort of idealized performance is enough for the linguist, because he is attempting to characterize the abstract, underlying form of linguistic knowledge, or competence. In the actual, human performance of speaking and understanding, many psychological variables intervene to distort behavioral predictions based on the pure competence model offered by linguists. For example, memory span keeps us from uttering or understanding sentences beyond a given length or level of complexity. Factors like fatigue, switching of attention, distractability, emotional excitement, drugs, and so on, affect linguistic performance in many ways not envisaged by the linguistic model of competence.

The linguist is not especially interested in the everyday use of language, but in the underlying ability which makes it possible for people (generally linguists) in ideal situations to make judgments of grammaticality, identify grammatical relations, and so on. Psychologists, however, have a double task: On one hand, we must try to cut through the maze of psychological factors that make performance deviate from competence in order to convince ourselves that competence, as described by the linguists, has "psychological reality"—that it exists in some psychological sense. On the other hand, however, we are also very much interested in just those psychological factors which do cause performance to deviate from competence. The sort of machine we are interested in is not only one which comes to linguistically acceptable conclusions under ideal conditions, but also one which makes human-like errors under less-than-ideal conditions.

In Chapter 2 you will read about some psycholinguistic experiments which have attempted to deal with problems of both competence and performance in the context of the psychological laboratory. First, though, we must consider the linguistic competence model in somewhat greater detail. As I have indicated repeatedly above, the model which I consider most relevant to psychology is that of transformational grammar. This sytem is extremely complex and is currently undergoing rapid change and modification. The most we can hope for in a brief introductory chapter of this sort is the barest outline of its major premises.[2] But, before approaching the complexities of transformational grammar, it would be useful to examine some of the alternative sorts of grammars which have been proposed as psychologically relevant, in order to convince ourselves that language is far more complex than it may appear at first blush.

PROBABILISTIC, LEFT-TO-RIGHT MODELS

The model of grammar which has most appealed to traditional behavioristic psychology is a left-to-right probabilistic model ("Markov process"), in which the occurrence of each word is determined by the immediately preceding word or series of words. This model is in consonance with associative chain theories of behavior, in which each response serves as a stimulus for the next response. In 1951, the noted neuropsychologist Karl Lashley published an important paper entitled "The Problem of Serial Order in Behavior," in which he presented strong arguments against associative chain theories in general. It is of interest that he based much of his argument on linguistic evidence.

Lashley points out, first of all, that there is no intrinsic order to words in themselves. Depending on what is said, a given word can be followed by a variety of words. He gives as an example the word pronounced *rite*, which has four spellings, many meanings, and can serve as noun, adjective, adverb, and verb. He says:

> In such a sentence as "The mill-wright on my right thinks it right that some conventional rite should symbolize the right of every man to write as he pleases," word arrangement is obviously not due to any direct association of the word "right" itself with other

---

[2]A valuable and readable introduction to transformational grammar has recently been published by Jacobs and Rosenbaum (1968). Postal (1964) has written a brief and readable introductory article. An excellent review of all of psycholinguistics, including a clear exposition of the fundamentals of transformational grammar, is given by Miller and McNeill (1969). The references in footnote 1 provide more advanced and technical orientations to the field.

words, but to meanings which are determined by some broader relations (in Saporta, 1961, p. 183).

Lashley concludes that there must be an underlying intention to say something, a "determining tendency," and that a "schema of order" is responsible for the serial order of words in the resulting utterance. He finds evidence for these notions in slips of the tongue and errors in type-writing. The most frequent errors are those of anticipation — using a word or letter sooner than it is required in the flow of speech or typing. Thus there must be an underlying level at which elements larger than words are being readied for production. He speaks of syntax as "not inherent in the words employed or in the idea to be expressed," but rather as "a gen-eralized pattern imposed upon the specific acts as they occur."

Further, he notes that word-to-word associations cannot account for the comprehension of speech any more than they can account for the pro-duction of speech. As an example, he offers the following sentence, which you should imagine as spoken rather than written: "Rapid righting with his uninjured hand saved from loss the contents of the capsized canoe." When listening to this sentence, the meaning of "righting" is not deter-mined until several seconds *after* it has been heard. It is a frequent phe-nomenon in language that the selection or understanding of words early in a sentence is determined by words coming later in the sentence. This phenomenon seems to have no place in an associative chain model of language.

These are several of the incisive arguments offered by Lashley in his now classic paper. They anticipate Chomsky's arguments against prob-abilistic models of grammar in *Syntactic Structures* (1957). There Chom-sky points out that the transitional probabilities between words in a string of words (i.e., the probability with which one word may follow another) have no relation to whether that string of words is a grammatical sen-tence. He offers the word string: "Colorless green ideas sleep furiously." The transitional probabilities between these words are nil; that is, you have probably never heard sequences such as "colorless green," "ideas sleep," etc. Yet most people would probably agree that this word string is a grammatical, though bizarre sentence. On the other hand, if this sen-tence is read backwards ("Furiously sleep ideas green colorless") it is no longer a sentence, though the transitional probabilities between the words remain insignificant.

What happens if we are careful to pick sequences of words which have a high probability of following one another? In the following string, the occurrence of each word is strongly determined by the preceding word: "Goes down here is not large feet are the happy days." Clearly, there is no guarantee that a sentence will be generated if each word is picked on the basis of its probability of following the immediately preceding word. Thus a probabilistic, left-to-right model is inadequate as a theory of grammar in that it fails to differentiate between sentences and nonsentences. The fact that a string of words is or is not a sentence is independent of the sequential probabilities between the words.

There is a deeper argument, however—and it is that a probabilistic, left-to-right model cannot even generate all of the grammatical sentences of English because we have the possibility of embedding sentences inside of other sentences. Chomsky has an excellent discussion of this entire matter in Chapter 3 of *Syntactic Structures*. On page 22 he points out that there are several forms of English sentences into which other sentences can be inserted. Taking S as a symbol for "sentence," we have such constructions as:

(18) If S_1, then S_2.

(19) Either S_1 or S_2.

(20) The man who said that S is arriving today.

For example, take the sentence, "The man who said S is here," where S is another sentence. This sentence could be rewritten as: "The man who said Chomsky has very weak arguments is here." In this example, the word "is" is dependent upon "man," which occurred much earlier. A Markov chain, in which each word is based on the immediately preceding word, cannot account for the transition between "arguments" and "is," or for the fact that "is" is really related to "man." Suppose we expanded the scope of our probabilistic chain, and allowed the choice of each successive word to be determined by the entire preceding chain, rather than just by the immediately preceding word. We would still have no basis for determining the occurrence of "is," because this word is dependent upon an element which appeared *before* the embedded sentence, and the probabilistic model has no way of recognizing this discontinuity. That is, it has no way of recognizing boundaries between phrases, clauses, or sentences.

The situation can get even more complicated—and not at all implausible—if we take the "if . . . then" construction and embed sentences within it. For example, I could say: "If the man who said that Chomsky has very weak arguments is here then either he has to defend his point or he has to be open to criticism."

This matter of discontinuous elements in sentences is a common grammatical device—probably used by all languages of the world. We find it not only in embedded sentences, but in verb + particle constructions (e.g., he *picked* the hat *up*; he *picked* the old hat *up*, etc.), in various auxiliary constructions (e.g., he *is* walking; he *has* walked), and so on.

The general point is simply this: In language there are many cases in which the choice of an element is determined by an element which occurred much earlier in the sentence. Thus it is not possible to explain sentence construction on the basis of a simple left-to-right model, in which each successive element is chosen on the basis of the immediately preceding element. It is necessary to *remember* what happened earlier in such sentences, and to keep track of such elements across gaps filled by intervening structures. (Note that there is no theoretical limit to the length of such intervening structures—e.g., a sentence of indeterminate length can be placed between "if" and "then.") This is Lashley's general argument about serial order in behavior, and why he introduced the notion of some underlying determining tendency. In our framework, this underlying structure must include an adequate grammar of the language.

There is another sort of argument against the attempt to account for the understanding of sentences simply on the basis of a knowledge of the ways in which words occur in sequence. Consider the sentence:

(21) They are visiting firemen.

This is an ambiguous sentence. It is ambiguous because we know something about its structure: We know that it really has two possible structures (in this case, two possible *surface* structures). One way of indicating this is by bracketing the groups of words which go together as phrases:

(21a) (they) ((are) (visiting firemen))
(21b) (they) ((are visiting) (firemen))

In terms of spelling or pronunciation these sentences are alike. In terms of grammar or meaning, however, they are quite different. Your knowledge of the two possible grammatical structures tells you that they have two different meanings. This is what transformationalists mean when they say that understanding a sentence is based upon knowledge of its structure. One way of representing this structure is by means of bracketing, as in (21a) and (21b) above. Another way is to draw a "tree" diagram:

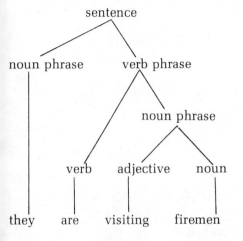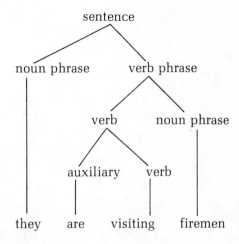

Note that there are several levels here. Human languages are organized in hierarchies of several levels. There are many levels of language: from discourse, to sentence, to phrase, to subphrase, to word, to word part, to meaningless separate sounds, to distinctive features of sounds. This brings us to the next sort of grammatical theory which we can try out for adequacy: "phrase structure grammar."

PHRASE STRUCTURE GRAMMAR

We say that we can understand sentence (21) in two ways because it has two *constituent structures*. That is to say, we can break it up into units, or constituents, in two different ways. Let me present a concrete example to clarify what linguists mean when they refer to constituent structures and to the sort of grammar involved in such analysis—phrase structure grammar.

Let us take a simple sentence which has been frequently used as an example (after Miller, 1962): "The boy hit the ball." Your linguistic intuition, or whatever you want to call it, tells you that some pairs of words are more closely related than other pairs. "The ball," for example, feels like a unit, but "hit the" does not. Another way to express this intuitive feeling is to say that "the ball" could easily be replaced by a single word—"it"—whereas "hit the" could not be easily replaced by another single word without changing the whole structure of the sentence. Likewise, "the boy" can be replaced by "he." This is shown on the second line of the diagram below. I think you will agree that "hit the ball" is a larger sort of unit, or constituent, which could be replaced by a more general word like "acted," as you see on the bottom line of the diagram.

The	boy	hit	the	ball
He		hit	it	
He		acted		

Linguists call this sort of process "constituent analysis." The segments of the sentences which can be treated as units are called its "constituents": "the ball" is a constituent, but "hit the" is not.

The procedure of constituent analysis is made more general by naming, or labelling, the different kinds of constituent units. For example,
using this sentence again, "the" is an article (T) and "boy" is a noun (N);
together they form a noun phrase (NP). "The ball" is thus also a noun
phrase (NP). The verb "hit" is combined with this noun phrase to form a
verb phrase (VP). At the highest level, the first noun phrase ("the boy")
combines with the verb phrase ("hit the ball") to make a grammatical
sentence. The names of the constituents can be introduced into the diagram:

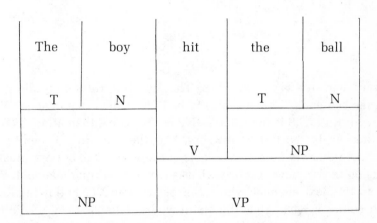

Abstract structured patterns such as these underlie grammatical sentences. There are various ways of notating such structures — so far you
have seen bracketing, tree diagrams, and box diagrams. Another way of
describing the constituent structure of a sentence is to use what is called
a *generative grammar*. This approach stems from ways of dealing with
combinatorial systems in formal logic. The idea here is to start with a
basic "axiom" (in our case, S, the symbol for "sentence") and apply
rules of formation which allow for the rewriting of the axiom until a sentence is derived. The way to test the acceptability of the rules is to see if
only grammatical sentences will be derived, or generated, in this way.
Any sentence which cannot be derived from such rules will, on a formal
basis, be considered ungrammatical. To make this concrete, let's see how
a small segment of English grammar — that dealing with the sort of sentence I've described above — might be expressed in this manner.

What you see below, greatly schematized and somewhat old-fashioned,
is the essence of a phrase structure grammar. There is a set of symbols of
the sort defined above (T, N, V, NP, VP) and rules of the sort of a → b,
where the arrow means "can be rewritten as."

Rules

1. S $\longrightarrow$ NP + VP

2. NP $\longrightarrow$ T + N

3. VP $\longrightarrow$ V + NP

4. T $\longrightarrow$ *the, a*

5. N $\longrightarrow$ *boy, girl, ball*

6. V $\longrightarrow$ *hit*

```
                    S
                  /   \
               NP      VP
              / \     /  \
             T   N   V    NP
             |   |   |   /  \
            the boy hit T    N
                       |    |
                      the  ball
```

We start with the basic axiom, S. The rewriting rules 1–6 allow us to form the sentence "The boy hit the ball" in a sequence of steps. Beginning with Rule 1, S is rewritten as NP + VP. Rule 2 then allows NP to be rewritten as T + N; Rule 4 rewrites T as *the*; and Rule 5 rewrites N as *boy*. Since there is no rule available for rewriting *the boy* we must stop at this point: We have reached what is called a *terminal element*. We go back to the next element which can be written: VP. Following Rule 3, this becomes V + NP. So at this point we have: *the boy* + V + NP. Rule 6 then allows us to rewrite V as *hit*, another terminal element. The only nonterminal element left now is NP, which, according to Rule 2 again, can be rewritten as T + N. Finally, using Rules 4 and 5 again, we can rewrite T + N as *the ball*, thus completing the possible application of rules in generating this sentence.

Note that we have two types of elements here. There are terminal elements (*the, a, boy, girl, ball, hit*), which means that there are no further rules for rewriting these elements. And there are nonterminal elements (S, NP, VP, T, N, V) which must be rewritten. We have formed a complete sentence when all of the elements are terminal.

Although this is a very simple example it has that all-important attribute of productivity which is so central to human language. You can see that we could generate such other sentences as "the boy hit the girl," "a girl hit a ball," and so on.

Chomsky has shown in Chapter 4 of *Syntactic Structures* that a grammar of the sort I have just described — a phrase structure grammar — overcomes one of the chief weaknesses of the Markov process models: It can handle embedded sentences. Since the phrase structure trees are constructed from top to bottom, rather than from left-to-right, at any point in the tree we can insert the symbol S again, which means sentence. This allows us to work out an entire sentence and go on to rewrite other non-terminal symbols in the tree once the branchings under the embedded S have all ended in terminal symbols.

In formal terms, we can have rewrite rules of the following types:

$S \rightarrow ab$

$S \rightarrow aSb$

Thus, if S can be rewritten as aSb, we can rewrite further, since S is not a terminal symbol, and we can get structures such as aabb. This is a very powerful sort of rule system, because it can generate an infinite set of sentences. The rules can be applied again and again: they have the feature known in mathematics and linguistics as "recursiveness." A person who has learned this small, finite set of rules would have the capacity, in principle, to deal with an infinite set of outputs of these rules. Here we have formulated a most central psychological aspect of linguistic competence: the ability of a finite set of rules to generate an infinite set of sentences.

A phrase structure grammar can thus deal with matters beyond the scope of a Markov process, left-to-right model. It can deal with embedded sentences, and, as in the example of "They are visiting firemen," it can deal with at least some ambiguous sentences by assigning different constituent structures to them. Such a grammar is also simpler from the point of view of the assumptions made about language development in childhood. In order to learn a grammar of the first type, a child would have to somehow compute the transitional probabilities between huge numbers of words. It has been estimated (Miller, Galanter, and Pribram, 1960) that human childhood is not long enough for such calculations to be carried out. In order to learn a phrase structure grammar, however, the child has to learn a vocabulary organized into classes (such as the traditional "parts of speech") and a set of rules for combining these categories into sentences. This is certainly far easier than learning all of the sequential probabilities of English words.

But it can still be argued whether a phrase structure grammar can account for everything we know about English. As I will try to explain next, transformationalists believe that such a grammar still leaves certain problems unaccounted for, and so they propose another set of rules of a new type. So far we have considered rules of formation; the next step will be to consider rules of transformation.

TRANSFORMATIONAL GRAMMAR

Now we must turn to some of the inadequacies of phrase structure grammar—but don't abandon this approach. These inadequacies motivated the invention of transformational grammar, which does not supplant phrase structure grammar, but adds another level to grammatical description. We will still need phrase structure grammar as a component of a total grammatical description of a language.

Phrase structure grammar is based on rules of formation which rewrite symbols into other symbols, like the rule: S → NP + VP. The additional level which Chomsky and his followers have developed is based on rules of transformation, which are rules for rearranging elements. For example, consider our familiar sentence and a corresponding question:

(22) The boy hit the ball.

(23) What did the boy hit?

These two sentences are obviously related, but phrase structure grammar does not reveal the relationship. How is the question (23) related to the declarative (22)? The question word "what" asks a question about the object of the verb "hit." In (22) the object of that verb is "the ball," and it follows the verb. In (23) there is no object, and the question word appears at the beginning of the sentence. Apparently, "the ball" and "what" play similar roles in relation to the verb in the two sentences. In transformational terms, a question of this sort is formed by replacing the object noun phrase by an appropriate question word and moving that question word to the front of the sentence. Note that the type of element which is rearranged, a noun phrase, is an element revealed by the constituent analysis procedures of phrase structure grammar. Thus it is clear that we will need two sorts of rules, and two levels of description, in a transformational grammar of a language: phrase structure rules generating deep structures, and transformational rules converting deep structures into surface structures.

Let us trace the sequence of steps taken thus far in transforming the declarative (22) into the question (23) (omitting many fine details). We have carried out the following operations: "The boy hit the ball" ⇒ "The boy hit what" ⇒ "What the boy hit?" This last sentence does not yet correspond to (23) (although it is the sort of question form typically uttered by two-year-olds at a certain stage of development). There is yet more transformational work to be done. Sentence (23) has an additional word, "did." Where did this word come from? Consider the following pair of sentences:

(24) The boy had hit the ball.

(25) What had the boy hit?

How does this pair of sentences differ from the former? The order of elements in the two questions, (23) and (25), is the same: question word – past tense auxiliary – noun phrase – verb. In the case of the latter pair, the past tense auxiliary ("had") is also present in the affirmative sentence. In this case, therefore, the sequence of steps is: "The boy had hit the ball" ⇒ "The boy had hit what" ⇒ "What the boy had

hit" ⇒ "What had the boy hit?" We have an extra step here—a step
which apparently was not present in the first case. After moving the
question word to the front it was necessary to invert the subject and auxiliary: "the boy had" ⇒ "had the boy." Formation of the question thus
requires at least three transformational operations: (1) replacement of
object noun phrase by "what," (2) preposing of "what," (3) transposing
of subject and auxiliary.

Now back to the problem of that word "did" which popped up in (23).
Two paragraphs back we were left stranded with the childish "What the
boy hit?" The next instruction is to transpose subject and auxiliary—but
there is no auxiliary. In this case, therefore, we have to introduce an auxiliary, the "dummy" auxiliary "do." This auxiliary is placed in its appropriate position before the subject, and it also takes on the past tense
of the verb, resulting in sentence (23).

This may sound complicated, but it is, in fact, a great simplification of
the actual transformational process. Note that we have accounted for the
puzzling intrusion of "did" in the first question. Can you explain the
presence of forms of "do" in other sentences related to sentence (22),
such as the following?

(26) The boy didn't hit the ball.
(27) What didn't the boy hit?
(28) Did the boy hit the ball?
(29) Didn't the boy hit the ball?
(30) The boy DID hit the ball.

An explanation of these sentences (which we will not undertake here)
reveals several important aspects of grammatical transformations: A
transformation is an operation which converts one phrase structure into
another. This is accomplished by such simple operations as *substitution*
("what" for "the ball"), *displacement* (preposing of "what"), *permuta-
tion* (of subject and auxiliary) and a few others. Such operations are linguistic universals, characteristic of all known human languages.

Another important aspect of transformational grammar is revealed in
sentence (22). Although that sentence has no apparent auxiliary, it must
have some abstract auxiliary in its underlying structure, since the auxiliary appears in the corresponding interrogative and negative sentences.
Thus, as pointed out earlier, not everything we know about a sentence is
revealed in the superficial string of words which are uttered aloud. This
distinction between underlying and superficial linguistic structure, or
"deep" and "surface" structure, is one of the major contributions of
transformational grammar—both to linguistics and to psychology. Some
additional examples may help clarify this important distinction.

An obvious example of the capacity to interpret sentences is your ability to discover the logical propositions underlying utterances: in simple

terms, who is doing what to whom? The active sentence "Police club demonstrators" has the same meaning as its corresponding passive "Demonstrators are clubbed by police." In each case, you are able to discern who is subject and who is object of the verb, though the word order is changed. Within phrase structure grammar, however, there is no way to determine the fact that these two sentences, although differing in surface structure, have the same underlying meaning.

Lest you think that only position in a surface sentence frame guides you in your interpretation, consider the following two passive sentences:

(31) They were blocked by police.

(32) They were blocked by force.

There seem to be no grounds within phrase structure grammar for assigning different representations to these two sentences. As far as phrase structure grammar is concerned, these two sentences have the same constituent structure. But we know that they are understood differently, and the grammar must account for this. Though "police" is the logical subject, or agent, of the first sentence, "force" does not play a similar syntactic role in the second. Your knowledge of English structure makes it clear that the second sentence omits mention of the agent, though you know he is a user of force. That is, the two sentences can be related to different paraphrases: (31) is related to "Police blocked them," while (32) is related to "Somebody blocked them by force." The sentences are understood differently because they have different "transformational histories." On the surface they have the same structure, but these structures are derived from different underlying, or deep, structures. The hallmark of transformational grammar is the emphasis on these two levels of sentence interpretation: the surface level, directly related to the sentence as it is heard, and the deep level, directly related to the meaning of the sentence. You had another example of this discrepancy in examples (11) and (12): "John is easy to please" and "John is eager to please."

Phrase structure grammar is also inadequate when faced with sentences like (15): "Visiting relatives can be a nuisance." A similar example is: "The shooting of the hunters was terrible." In sentences like these there is no basis for assigning two different immediate constituent analyses, nor is there any word in the sentence which can be said to have two different meanings. Again, one must look to deep structural differences.

The difference between deep and surface structure is revealed in many other ways. As a final example, consider the sentence:

(33) John was looking the word up.

There must be some way of indicating that "look up" is a unit—that these two words are part of the verb, though they do not occur contiguously in the surface structure, and that "was" and "-ing" likewise go

together. It would take a tangled tree diagram to express these relationships!

There are many, many such examples. Transformationalists are very
good at finding them, and their writings are full of clever and intriguing
tidbits of this sort. But, most importantly, facts like these have led Chomsky to say:

> It is clear, in short, that the surface structure is often misleading
> and uninformative and that our knowledge of language involves
> properties of a much more abstract nature, not indicated directly
> in the surface structure. Furthermore, even such artificially simple
> examples as these show how hopeless it would be to try to account
> for linguistic competence in terms of "habits," "dispositions,"
> "knowing how," and other concepts associated with the study of
> behavior, as this study has been circumscribed, quite without war-
> rant, in recent years (1968, p. 32).

The sort of linguistic competence referred to here is a system of rules
which relates semantic interpretations of sentences to their acoustic
phonetic representations. That is to say, syntax is a device which relates
sounds and meanings. Such a model has important psychological implications. If the meanings of utterances are not directly expressed in the
sounds which we hear, then psychology must develop a rich cognitive
theory of the inner mental structures which make it possible to utter and
comprehend sentences. This theory cannot deal with observable "stimuli" and "responses" alone, because all of the information for the processing of speech is not present in observable behavior. And developmental psychologists cannot speak of language acquisition by children in
terms of such variables as "imitation" and "reinforcement" alone, for
what the child learns is not a set of utterances, but a set of rules for processing utterances. These issues will be considered in greater detail in the
following two chapters.

The discussion in this chapter has dealt mainly with the syntactic
component of transformational grammar. We have been concerned with
the deep and surface structures of sentences. The grammar has two other
components, which we will not take up in detail here. There is a phonological component, which converts surface structures into the sound patterns of spoken utterances. This component has recently been described
in detail by Chomsky and Halle (1968), and is mentioned only briefly in
reference to the child's development of phonology in Chapter 3. The
other major component, the semantic component, has yet to receive an
entirely satisfactory description. This component relates deep structures
to meanings. Questions of semantics are currently hotly debated in trans-

formational grammar. The relations of syntax and semantics will doubt-less be a major focus of new development in linguistics in the seventies. (Several problems of semantics are discussed in Chapter 4.)

To conclude this very rapid overview of a very complex field, here is Chomsky's summary of the basic nature of a transformational generative grammar. This characterization is believed to be applicable to all human languages.

> The grammar as a whole can thus be regarded, ultimately, as a de-vice for pairing phonetically represented signals with semantic interpretations, this pairing being mediated through a system of abstract structures generated by the syntactic component. Thus the syntactic component must provide for each sentence (actually, for each interpretation of each sentence) a semantically interpret-able *deep structure* and a phonetically interpretable *surface struc-ture*, and, in the event that these are distinct, a statement of the relation between these two structures. . . . Roughly speaking, it seems that this much structure is common to all theories of gen-erative grammar, or is at least compatible with them. Beyond this loose and minimal specification, however, important differences emerge (1964, p. 52).

2

Psycholinguistic Investigations of Grammar

Just as we induce a three-dimensional space underlying the two-dimensional pattern on the retina, so we must induce a syntactic structure underlying the linear string of sounds in a sentence. And just as the student of space perception must have a good understanding of projective geometry, so a student of psycholinguistics must have a good understanding of grammar.

—George A. Miller (1962, p. 756)

By now you have a vague idea of the nature of grammatical description, and we are ready to consider some aspects of the psychological status of this sort of analysis. The problem is one of drawing behavioral implications from the theories of language advanced by linguists. At the beginning of the past decade a summary of psycholinguistic investigations of grammar could have been quickly and easily made. In 1962 about all that was in print was George Miller's review of pilot work at the Center for Cognitive Studies at Harvard University. Now, however, it is impossible to review all of the published research in this area—let alone the unpublished reports which circulate in an "underground" network of progress reports, technical reports, annual reports, dittoed reports, mimeographed reports, and so on. The most that can be accomplished here is an overview of some of the major techniques which have been used and the types of problems at which they have been directed.[1]

In attempting to use a formal grammatical theory as a model for human language behavior we must bear in mind—as has been repeatedly emphasized—the distinction between competence and performance. The formal theory can merely be assumed to exist somehow and somewhere in the brain of the language-user, determining his ability to perform in certain ways. Linguistic competence is thus a model of what is assumed to exist in the mind of the speaker—a model built by the linguist on the basis of his intuitive ability to discriminate well-formed from ill-formed utterances, etc. The plausibility of its existence can be assessed only through a careful study of the actual performance which it is believed to determine. Any behavior as complex as human linguistic behavior, however, must be influenced by a variety of factors. To the extent that performance is predictable from a theory of competence, the plausibility of that theory is enhanced; and, by deviating in regular fashion from the base-line predictions of that theory, linguistic performance may reveal important psychological factors involved in the passage from competence to performance. This means that we must be especially careful in designing our

---

[1]A number of reviews of psycholinguistic research are currently available to the interested reader. Among them are Ervin-Tripp and Slobin (1966), Lyons and Wales (1966), Miller and McNeill (1969). An excellent paperback anthology of papers on psycholinguistics has been prepared by Oldfield and Marshall (1968).

psycholinguistic experiments, because, if our subjects do not perform the way the theory predicts, we want to know whether this is because the theory is wrong, or because psychological factors are responsible for *systematic deviations* from the predictions.

Accordingly, there have been two interlocking goals of psycholinguistic investigations of grammar: (1) assessment of the "psychological reality" of the linguistic description of competence and (2) determination of the psychological factors which influence linguistic performance and definition of the nature of this influence. The research reviewed in this chapter deals with adult verbal behavior, while the following chapter discusses the acquisition of grammar by children.

Psycholinguistic investigations of grammar deal with both phrase structure and transformational issues. On the phrase structure level one can seek evidence that people break up sentences into constituent structures or phrases as defined by linguistics. On the transformational level questions have been asked in regard to a number of problems:

(1) Relations between sentence types: Let us say that the grammar gives us a metric for distances between sentences — for example, a measure that Sentence C is, in some sense, further from Sentence A than is Sentence B. Does this mean that it should take more time or effort to go from C to A than from B to A? (Cf. Miller and McKean, 1964.)

(2) Complexity and sentence processing: If Sentence B is considered more complex than Sentence A, does this mean that Sentence B should be more difficult to *understand* and/or *remember* than Sentence A? There are several variables here which have to be further defined. *Complexity* can be interpreted in many ways: embedding, direction of branching, number of rules in derivation, etc. *Memory* can be defined in terms of recall or recognition. And *understanding* can be measured in terms of the time it takes to understand a sentence and in terms of the accuracy of understanding — in psychological terms, we can speak of response times and errors. (Cf. Slobin, 1966a.)

(3) Grammaticality: Does the sense of grammaticality demonstrated by subjects in experiments correspond with the linguists' definitions of grammaticality? How do subjects deal with semigrammatical sentences?

(4) Deep and surface structure: What evidence is there that both of these levels are involved in sentence processing? Is it psychologically valid to postulate two levels of syntactic structure? (Cf. Rohrman, 1968.)

Only a few examples of some of these research directions are presented here. However, before discussing specific experiments, it would be useful to say a few words about the point of this sort of research. I think it is legitimate for psychologists to try to determine the nonlinguistic psychological variables which may influence linguistic performance. But why should we psychologists bother devising experiments to check the psychological reality of linguistic descriptions formulated by linguists? Can't we just take the linguists' word that they have devised appropriate descriptions? Many linguists would answer this last question by saying: "Yes, leave the description of language to us. It's not the sort of thing that can be determined by psychological experiment."

Chomsky has succinctly discussed this issue in a number of places (e.g., 1964, pp. 79–81), and emphasizes that grammars are best constructed on the basis of introspective judgments, occasionally corroborated by other speakers. He would evaluate grammars on the basis of their general and systematic ability to account for linguistic observations in a coherent and elegant manner. He leaves a small opening for psycholinguistics: "Operational tests that consistently supported introspective judgment in clear cases would, were they available, also be relevant in determining the correctness of particular observations" (1964, p. 80). In fact, Chomsky has spoken approvingly of some of the experiments you will read about shortly. He approves of them because they substantiate the obvious – that is, they are independent, operational measures of facts which he, as a linguist, has already proven to his satisfaction. He argues that if such tests were available and reliable – and valid in clear cases – he would be willing to use them to decide unclear cases. In other words, though our tests may still be rather crude, someday we may be able to serve as "toolmaker to the linguist."

It is encouraging to know that someday we may be of use to linguists in the complex work they undertake. But psychologists have another interest in these operational tests – even if they substantiate what is obvious to the linguist. This interest might be called "ideological," or perhaps "temperamental." Psychologists generally don't want to believe "obvious things" until they can make them happen themselves in their own laboratories and subject them to the standards of evidence which they have come to accept. Maybe this reflects psychologists' needs for manipulation and control; or maybe psychologists have to "learn by doing"; or maybe psychologists only accept facts presented in a certain framework of terminology and methodology; or maybe (as many of them would like to believe) psychologists have "higher" or "more valid" criteria for truth. Often the scientific ideology of psychology has blinded its practitioners to important issues and important sources of evidence. Perhaps even much of the research in psycholinguistics serves merely to "soothe the scientific conscience," as Chomsky puts it (1964, p. 81). I leave it to you to interpret and assess our needs and motives, and the value of our experimental results. At any rate, you may find some of the experiments engaging in their own right – and maybe that's why we spend our time doing them.

PERCEPTION OF CONSTITUENT STRUCTURE

A basic assumption of linguistics, as noted in Chapter 1, is that sentences are not merely strings of words, but *structured* strings of words consisting of hierarchies of units. This notion of constituent, or phrase structure of sentences has been brought into the psychological laboratory by Fodor, Bever, and Garrett at MIT (Fodor and Bever, 1965; Garrett, Bever, and Fodor, 1966). These researchers devised an ingenious technique for revealing the presence of phrase boundaries in the perception of sentences. The technique is based on the Gestalt assumption that a perceptual unit tends "to preserve its integrity by resisting interruptions" (Fodor and Bever, 1965, p. 415). In the experiment of Fodor and Bever, subjects listened to a sentence during which a click occurred, and immediately afterward were required to write down the sentence and indicate where the click had occurred. If a phrase is a perceptual unit, subjects should tend to hear a click which occurred during a phrase as having occurred between phrases.

One of their sentences was: "That he was happy was evident from the way he smiled." This sentence has a major break between "happy" and "was." A click was placed at various positions in this sentence, as indicated by the asterisks below:

That he was happy was evident from the way he smiled.
　　 * *　 *　 *　 *　　 * ** *

Each subject heard the sentence with only one click in it.

Fodor and Bever found that subjects were most accurate in locating the click which occurred between the two major phrases of the sentence—i.e., between "happy" and "was" in the above example. Clicks occurring before this break tended to be displaced towards the right (i.e., into the break), and those occurring after the break towards the left (i.e., again into the break). Fodor and Bever conclude that their findings "appear to demonstrate that the major syntactic break plays an important role in determining the subjective location of noises perceived during speech," thus supporting the hypothesis that "the unit of speech perception corresponds to the constituent."

One might call these results into question on the suspicion that the major syntactic break is signalled by some acoustic means, such as pause. In additional research, however, Garrett, Bever, and Fodor (1966) have demonstrated that there are no clear acoustic cues which mark the breaks between constituent phrases. The most dramatic evidence of this surprising fact comes from an experiment comparing pairs of sentences such as:

(1) As a result of their invention's *influence the company was given*
    an award.　　　　　　　　　　　　　　　　　　 *　　　 *

(2) The chairman whose methods still *influence the company was given an award.*   *   *

When subjects were asked where they hear the longest pause in these sentences, they report—as one might expect—that they hear a pause in (1) between "influence" and "the," and in (2) between "company" and "was." The perceived pause thus corresponds to the major constituent boundaries in the two sentences.

The ingenious part of the experiment comes next. The two sentences were recorded on tape, and the two italicized segments were interchanged. That is, the last part of sentence (2) was spliced onto the beginning of sentence (1), and vice versa. *Subjects' perception of pause location, however, was unchanged.* The same is true of click displacement. As indicated by asterisks in the two sentences above, a click occurred either during "company" or "was." The perception of click location, however, was significantly different for the two sentences. The click in sentence (1) tended to be heard between "influence" and "the," and in (2) between "company" and "was." But remember: the sentences were acoustically identical! Thus it seems that a listener perceives a sentence on the basis of his analysis of its constituent structure, and not because of a special acoustic cue to segmentation.

This finding is extremely significant, and is reflected again and again in studies of speech perception (cf. Liberman et al., 1967). It seems that the hearer assigns a perceptual structure to speech sounds on the basis of his knowledge of the rules of language. The perceiver is thus an *active* interpreter of the acoustic speech signals which he receives.

MEMORY FOR SENTENCES

Much psycholinguistic research has been concerned with the question of how sentences are represented in memory and with the limitations imposed by human memory upon sentence processing. It seems clear that sentences have some special status in memory. People do not simply remember a sentence as a string of words, because it is easier to recall a particular sentence than a randomization of the same string. In addition, anomalous sentences are more difficult to recall and recognize than are normal, meaningful sentences. Syntactic structure and meaning thus play important roles in memory for speech. Furthermore, a short while after hearing a sentence, a person can repeat the general meaning of that sentence although he may have forgotten the particular details of its structure; that is, he can paraphrase or summarize what he has recently heard—often without realizing that he has failed to give a verbatim report. Thus it seems also clear that meaning and form can be stored independently, and that the underlying meaning of a sentence is more persistent in memory than the surface structure in which that meaning is expressed. All of these generalizations are the subject of intensive, ongoing research in psycholinguistics. The experiments discussed below are representative of some of this research.

Memory Span

It has become clear from a number of studies that memory span for sentences is not determined so much by the number of words in a sentence as by the grammatical structure of the sentence. Miller and Isard (1964), for example, carried out an experiment in which subjects had to memorize sentences, all 22 words in length, but of varying degrees of self-embedding. Here is an example of successive degrees of self-embedding from their study:

[0] She liked the man that visited the jeweler that made the ring that won the prize that was given at the fair.

[1] The man that she liked visited the jeweler that made the ring that won the prize that was given at the fair.

[2] The jeweler that the man that she liked visited made the ring that won the prize that was given at the fair.

[3] The ring that the jeweler that the man that she liked visited made won the prize that was given at the fair.

[4] The prize that the ring that the jeweler that the man that she liked visited made won was given at the fair.

It is evident that the last two sentences are quite difficult to read and understand, let alone remember. Miller and Isard found that their subjects could easily remember sentences with one or two relative clauses, but memorization of sentences with three or four self-embedded relative clauses was difficult for all subjects. All five sentences are equally grammatical, and equally long, but they differ in the burden they place on immediate memory. The problem is posed by discontinuous constituents: the nouns which occur early in the sentence are related to verbs which occur late in the sentence. Thus short-term memory span is an extremely important performance variable. As Miller and Isard put it, "our capacity to deal with interruptions may be extremely limited" (p. 292).

Memory Storage of Syntactic Information

Savin and Perchonock (1965) conducted an experiment which attempted to show how certain aspects of syntax are used in remembering sentences. We have noted that the units in which a subject encodes and recalls a sentence are larger than individual words. Savin and Perchonock demonstrated the role of syntax in organizing sentences into units larger than words.

Their idea, based on transformational grammar, was that a sentence can be divided into an underlying proposition plus some additional information about syntactic structure. For example, consider the following sentences:

ACTIVE: The boy has hit the ball.
PASSIVE: The ball has been hit by the boy.
NEGATIVE: The boy has not hit the ball.
PASSIVE NEGATIVE: The ball has not been hit by the boy.

All four of these sentences contain an underlying proposition about a boy having hit a ball. In addition, each of the sentences has a particular syntactic structure, as indicated by the labels preceding each sentence. The last sentence, for example, is both passive and negative. Savin and Perchonock predicted that such "grammatical tags" as "passive," "negative," and "question" would take up space in immediate memory.

To test this prediction, they had subjects memorize sentences of various grammatical types, each sentence followed by a list of words, which was also to be memorized. Their procedure is most clearly spelled out in their own words:

> On a typical trial, the S heard a sentence followed by a string of eight words. He was instructed to recall the sentence verbatim and then recall as many as possible of the words. He was allowed as much time as he wished to complete the recall; the next trial would not begin until he indicated that he was ready for it. The sentences were read with normal intonation; there was a 5-sec pause between the end of a sentence and the beginning of the list. The words on the list were read at the rate of 3/4 sec per word. All material was tape-recorded (1965, p. 350).

The independent variable was the number of words remembered after sentences of a given grammatical type. The idea is that the fewer words a subject recalls after a sentence, the more space in immediate memory is taken up by that sentence. Since the sentences varied, mainly in grammatical structure, the number of words recalled can be taken as a measure of the space taken up in immediate memory by grammar. The results are clear and dramatic. You can see them in Table 1.

Table 1 shows that the more complex the structure of the sentence, the fewer words are recalled in addition to the sentence. Furthermore, the order of difficulty of the sentence types matches that predicted by transformational grammar. It is evident that the number of words in a sentence is not the most important determiner of how much space it will occupy in

TABLE 1: MEAN NUMBER OF WORDS RECALLED AFTER EACH OF THE SENTENCE-TYPES[1]

Sentence Type	Example	Mean No. of Words Recalled
ACTIVE DECLARATIVE	The boy has hit the ball.	5.27
WH-QUESTION	What has the boy hit?	4.78
QUESTION	Has the boy hit the ball?	4.67
PASSIVE	The ball has been hit by the boy.	4.55
NEGATIVE	The boy has not hit the ball.	4.44
NEGATIVE QUESTION	Has the boy not hit the ball?	4.39
EMPHATIC	The boy *has* hit the ball.	4.30
NEGATIVE PASSIVE	The ball has not been hit by the boy.	3.48
PASSIVE QUESTION	Has the ball been hit by the boy?	4.02
NEGATIVE PASSIVE QUESTION	Has the ball not been hit by the boy?	3.85
EMPHATIC PASSIVE	The ball *has* been hit by the boy.	3.74

From *Journal of Verbal Learning and Verbal Behavior*, Copyright 1965, reprinted by permission of Academic Press, Inc. and the authors.
[1]Adapted from Savin and Perchonock (1965, p. 351).

memory. What is important is the structure of the sentence. For example, compare ACTIVE DECLARATIVE with WH-QUESTION. The former ("The boy has hit the ball") has six words; the latter ("What has the boy hit?") has only five. Yet the latter is more complex syntactically. As was noted in Chapter 1, in order to change the active declarative into a question you have to replace the object of the verb ("ball") by a wh-question word ("what"), and place that question word at the beginning of the sentence. This is a fairly complex grammatical transformation, and it is reasonable to expect that it should take up some additional space in memory. In fact, this is what Table 1 shows. Although the active declarative sentence is longer, subjects remember, on the average, 5.27 words in addition to this sort of sentence, while they only remember an average of 4.78 words after the shorter wh-question sentence. Also striking is a comparison of ACTIVE DECLARATIVE with EMPHATIC. These two sentences have the identical number of words. But in order to make a sentence emphatic, special stress must be placed at a given place in the sentence —namely on the first auxiliary (in this case, "has"). Although subjects remember 5.27 words after the simple declarative, they remember only 4.30 words after the same sentence with extra stress on the auxiliary for emphasis.

On the basis of lengthy data analysis, Savin and Perchonock conclude that: "Various grammatical features of English sentences — negative and passive transformations, and others — are encoded in immediate memory apart from one another, and apart from the rest of the sentence. The evidence for this claim is that sentences having these features require a larger part of the capacity of immediate memory than do otherwise identical sentences lacking these same features" (p. 348). The importance of this finding for psycholinguistics is the fact that people apparently hear and remember sentences in terms of their knowledge of the grammar of the language, and that this knowledge seems to be something like that described by transformational grammar.

Psychological Reality of Underlying Structure

The Savin and Perchonock experiment shows that grammatical information can take up space in memory. Other research on memory for sentences shows that sentences are remembered more in terms of their deep structures than their surface structures. Such research lends psychological support to the notion of deep and surface structure. For example, Arthur Blumenthal, at Harvard, has devised a technique of "prompted recall" to assess what parts of the deep structure of a sentence are most salient. In one experiment (1967) subjects were required to remember lists of two types of passive sentences:

(1) Gloves were made by tailors.
(2) Gloves were made by hand.

These two sentences have the same surface structure, but different deep structures. Underlying (1) is an assertion that tailors make gloves; underlying (2) is an assertion that somebody makes gloves, and that this process is done by hand.

Blumenthal aided subjects in recalling sentences by giving them the final noun ("tailors" or "hand") as a prompt. He found that nouns corresponding to the underlying subject ("tailors") were much more successful memory aids than nouns like "hand," which are not part of the basic underlying structure, but come from an adverbial phrase ("by hand") tacked onto that structure. The initial noun, "gloves," functions as object in both structures, and functions equally well as a prompt for both kinds of sentences.

In a later experiment, Blumenthal and Boakes (1967) used sentences like "John is eager to please" and "John is easy to please," in which the first word functions either as logical subject or logical object. Using the initial word as prompt for the recall of sentences such as these, they found that "words functioning as logical subjects were significantly more effective prompts than words functioning as logical objects." The difference in recall must be attributed to the differing functions which the prompt words perform in the underlying structures of these sentences, since they seem to have no significant difference in terms of their surface positions. These experiments make it quite clear that sentence processing must take place on two levels, as described in current linguistic theory.

Recoding in Memory

As pointed out above, while we generally remember quite well what we have just heard, we often cannot repeat it in the same words in which it was given. Apparently we quickly unravel the meaning and forget the syntax. This seems to support the notion that it is the underlying structure, rather than the surface details, which determines sentence meaning. This phenomenon has been nicely demonstrated by Jacqueline Sachs in a doctoral dissertation at the University of California, Berkeley (1967). She set out to demonstrate that: "Form which is not relevant to the meaning is normally not retained."

Her subjects listened to 28 passages of connected discourse. After each passage the subject was given a test sentence which was either identical to a sentence he had heard in the passage, or had been changed in either form or meaning. There were three delay intervals between the original sentence and the test sentence: no delay, 80 syllables (about 27 seconds), and 160 syllables (about 46 seconds). The subject never knew what sentence he would be tested on. The following are examples of the changes used in the experiment:

Original sentence: He sent a letter about it to Galileo, the great Italian scientist.

Semantic change: Galileo, the great Italian scientist, sent him a letter about it.

Active to passive change: A letter about it was sent to Galileo, the great Italian scientist.

Formal change: He sent Galileo, the great Italian scientist, a letter about it.

When the test sentence was heard with no intervening delay, subjects were able to recognize both semantic and syntactic changes. After only 80 syllables (about 27 seconds) of delay, subjects' recognition of syntactic changes (active-passive and other formal changes) was close to chance, while their recognition of semantic changes remained strong even after 160 syllables (about 46 seconds). In another study (unpublished), Sachs found that recognition for formal changes dropped to chance level after as short a delay as 40 syllables (7.5 seconds). It is clear that the formal structure of sentences is stored for only a brief period of time. A small change in wording which is related to meaning, however, is easily detected. For example, subjects recognized the following change in meaning with ease after 80 syllables of interpolated material: "There he met an archaeologist, Howard Carter, who urged him to join in the search for the tomb of King Tut," changed to: "There he met an archaeologist, Howard Carter, and urged him to join in the search for the tomb of King Tut." However, the following formal change in the original sentence was almost never noted: "There he met an archaeologist, Howard Carter, who urged that he join in the search for the tomb of King Tut.:

Sachs concludes that:

> . . . very slight changes in the words of a sentence had vastly different effects on the experimental task, depending on whether or not the change affected the meaning. . . .
>
> The findings . . . are consistent with a theory of comprehension which contends that the meaning of the sentence is derived from the original string of words by an active, interpretive process. That original sentence which is perceived is rapidly forgotten, and the memory then is for the information contained in the sentence (1967, p. 422).

Theoretical Implications

Immediate memory thus limits our ability both to recall and to recognize the form of sentences. Miller and Chomsky (1963) have suggested that such immediate memory limitations are intimately related to the fact that language has a transformational structure. By now it should be familiar to you that, according to the transformational model, syntax operates on two levels: a surface level related to the phonological structure of a sentence, and a deep level related to its semantic interpretation. Why should it be necessary to have these two levels? No invented language — such as computer languages, mathematics, etc. — has this dual structure of deep and surface levels. Perhaps natural language has this peculiar structure because it must be transmitted through the auditory medium — a medium which requires temporal order and rapid fading of message elements. Artificial languages are transmitted in a visual medium, and they can be scanned back and forth, but you can't look back at a sentence you've just heard for longer than it can linger in immediate memory (in the "echo box," as Miller once put it). Miller and Chomsky propose that there are two memories: short- and long-term. In short-term memory you have time only to compute the surface structure of a sentence, which is then sent to a larger memory store. There, without the immediate pressure of rapid fading, the deep structure and corresponding semantic interpretation are derived. (They are referring here, of course, to sentences which you *hear*.) Linguistic evidence for this notion is found in the fact that the syntactic structures on the surface level are much less complex than those on the deep level. Perhaps this is because the surface structures have to be computed under immediate time pressures. The thrust of this argument is that we *must* have a transformational grammar be-*cause* language is transmitted in the rapidly fading auditory mode.

This intriguing suggestion is certainly compatible with the experimental data on memory for sentences presented above.[2]

UNDERSTANDING OF SENTENCES

The experiments on memory for sentences have begun to clarify the complexities of sentence processing, and demonstrate the fruitful interaction of linguistic analysis and psychological experimentation in defining major variables involved in linguistic performance. We have yet to ask, however, how people deal with sentences when they are required, explicitly, to understand them. In the experiments discussed below, subjects are asked to respond to the meaning of a sentence. This allows us to look for interactions between form and meaning.

In the early stages of this sort of research it was hoped that speed and/or accuracy of comprehension of sentences of various grammatical types would provide a reliable metric of their syntactic complexity. For example, since active sentences are syntactically less complex than passives, it was thought that they should be understood more efficiently. A similar expectation was held in regard to the relative complexity of affirmative and negative sentences, and so on. The search for a reliable metric of syntactic complexity, however, has not been strikingly successful, and the reason for this failure is an important one. We soon discovered that understanding a sentence can depend as much upon the context in which it is used as upon its syntactic form. That is, one cannot speak of the complexity of processing a sentence of a given grammatical form in the abstract. Sentences are used to express meanings in situations, and language allows for a range of syntactic expressions because they are called for in a range of communicative contexts. In the experiments described below you will see that a passive sentence need not always be more difficult to understand than an active, and that a negative need not always be more difficult than an affirmative. Rather it seems that people prefer to describe certain types of situations using certain types of sentences.

---

[2]For related studies on memory for sentences see Mehler (1963), Slobin (1968), and numerous papers to appear in Weksel and Bever (in press).

Before the work on transformational grammar began in psychology, processes of sentence understanding were studied by the British psychologist Peter Wason in his investigations of psychological aspects of negation (1959, 1961). In one of his experiments (1961), subjects were presented with simple affirmative and negative sentences and were asked to decide whether each sentence was true or false. The sentences were of the form: "N (is, is not) an (even, odd) number"· where N is a digit in the range 2 – 9, and parentheses indicate alternative sentence frames. Thus four sentence types were used: (1) true affirmatives (e.g., "Eight is an even number"), (2) false affirmatives (e.g., "Nine is an even number"), (3) true negatives (e.g., "Nine is not an even number"), and (4) false negatives (e.g., "Eight is not an even number"). Wason found that subjects took longer and made more errors on the negative statements than on the affirmative statements. It is likely that such negative statements are difficult to verify unless they are compared with affirmative statements. Similar findings were reported for Hebrew-speaking subjects (Eifermann, 1961). In such experiments it seems that negative sentences are difficult to process not because of their syntactic form but because of the way they must be used in the task at hand. The difficulty seems more a conceptual than a syntactic one.

This interpretation is supported by more recent work in which Wason has shown that, in some contexts, negatives are actually quite easy to process quickly and correctly. Negatives are apparently easiest to deal with (and most commonly used) in the context of "plausible denial" – that is, it is more plausible to deny that a spider is an insect than to deny that a pig is an insect. In Wason's words: "The statement to a child, 'a whale is not a fish,' would usually be more illuminating than the statement, 'a herring is not an animal.' A whale *might* be wrongly classified as a fish, but a herring would hardly be classified as an animal. Similarly, the statement, 'the train was not late this morning,' would obviously be more pertinent when the train is normally late than when it is normally punctual" (p. 8). In a clever experiment, which is too complex to report in detail here, Wason (1965) showed that negatives used to make plausible denials can be produced as quickly and easily as some affirmatives. For example, if you have an array of seven red circles and one blue circle, it is easier to say of the one exceptional blue circle that it is not red (plausible denial) than it is to say that one of the red circles is not blue (implausible denial). Furthermore, a plausible denial in regard to the exceptional circle ("That circle is not red") can be produced as quickly as an affirmative statement in regard to an unexceptional circle ("That circle is red"). Thus, the context facilitates the use of a negative utterance if it functions to make a plausible denial. Experiments of this sort make it clear that semantic and pragmatic factors must be considered along with syntactic variables in a full description of the ways in which people deal with sentences in real situations.

Similar conclusions come from experiments in which subjects are asked to determine whether a given sentence is true or false with respect to a picture of a situation (Gough, 1965, 1966; McMahon, 1963; Slobin, 1963, 1966a). In these experiments subjects were asked to determine the truth values of four types of sentences with regard to pictured or imagined referent situations: active affirmative, passive affirmative, negative, and passive negative. The general finding in these studies was that passive sentences required more time to evaluate than active sentences; that negative sentences required more time than affirmatives (either active or passive); and that passive negatives were the most difficult to evaluate. The studies also made it possible to determine the amount of time required to deal with the features of passivity and negativity. In comparing response time to active and passive sentences, one can determine the amount of extra time required to deal with the passive. Likewise, one can determine the extra time required to deal with the negative aspect of sentences by comparing response times to negative and affirmative sentences. If these two syntactic features, passive and negative, are dealt with separately in sentence processing, one might expect that the extra time required to evaluate passive negative sentences should be the sum of the extra time required for dealing with passivity and the extra time required for dealing with negativity. In fact, this was generally the case: the sums of the additional times required to evaluate negatives and to evaluate passives, in comparison with active declaratives, roughly corresponded to the additional time required to evaluate passive negatives. This is in consonance with the notion that the passive negative is a composite of a negative and a passive transformation. However, it is important to note that passive affirmatives are easier to comprehend than negatives, although they seem to be more complex syntactically. When subjects are required to comprehend a sentence the important variable seems to be whether the sentence is affirmative or negative, as shown by Wason and Eifermann. There is apparently something difficult about deciding if a negative statement is true or false.

Studies of comprehension make it evident that more than syntax is involved in real-life sentence processing. In fact, the role of syntax can be quite dramatically altered by manipulating the meaningful purposes to which sentences can be put. For example, in some experiments (Slobin, 1963, 1966a) it was possible to manipulate the semantics of the situation in such a way as to eliminate the distinction between active and passive in terms of processing difficulty. That is, there are some cases in which passives are no harder to understand than actives. These are situations in which it is clear from the semantics of the sentences which noun is the subject and which the object. In a sentence like "The cat is being chased by the dog," either noun could logically serve as the subject of the sentence. Such sentences can be called *reversible*, since they can be reversed and still be normal English sentences (e.g., "The dog is being chased by the cat"). Passive forms of reversible sentences are, indeed, harder to understand than their corresponding actives. Apparently, part of the difficulty in understanding the passive lies in figuring out which noun is the subject. But it is also possible, in experiments on sentence verification, to use pictures which are described by *nonreversible* sentences. For example, the sentence, "The boy is raking the leaves" cannot be reversed without producing an anomalous sentence, "The leaves are raking the boy." This is a nonreversible sentence. Passive versions of sentences like this—"The leaves are being raked by the boy" —are no harder to understand than actives. Again, it seems that part of the difficulty of understanding a sentence is based on its semantics. Here there is no problem in figuring out which noun is the subject of the sentence, and so the passive form of this sort of sentence presents no special comprehension problems to subjects.

The entire collection of experiments on sentence comprehension (including others not reviewed here) leads to an interesting point, which must be considered in the light of the history of psycholinguistic research. Earlier it had been held by many psycholinguists (e.g., Miller, 1962) that simple active declarative sentences were somehow "psychologically central." They were short, had a minimum of grammatical transformations in their derivation, and seemed to be used most efficiently in various experimental tasks. It seems more reasonable to propose, however, that different sentence types are used to describe different types of situations. Wason pointed out the use of negative to deny plausible misconceptions. Passives are also used in special situations. Indeed, the passive sentence has been the subject of a rather large number of psycholinguistic experiments and speculations (e.g., Clark, 1965; Hayhurst, 1967; Sachs, 1967; Slobin, 1966a, 1968; Turner and Rommetveit, 1967a, 1967b, 1968).

These investigations highlight the suggestion made above that passives may be appropriate and normal to certain contexts. For example, the passive is used in English to emphasize the object of action by mentioning it at the beginning of the sentence (e.g., "The treaty was ratified by the Senate"). In a recent study, Turner and Rommetveit (1968) revealed the emphasis function of the passive by directing subjects' attention in remembering active and passive sentences. This was done by presenting pictures together with sentences, and later using pictures as prompts for aiding the recall of sentences. The picture showed either the actor, the object of action, or the total situation referred to by the sentence. When used as retrieval prompts, pictures of actor or total situation facilitated recall of active sentences, while pictures of object of action facilitated recall of passive sentences. Active sentences tended to be recalled as passives when a picture of the object served as a recall prompt, while pictures of actor or total situation facilitated recall of passives as actives. Thus, focussing attention on the object of action encourages subjects to refer to the object first. Such focussing requires, of course, that the sentence be phrased in the passive voice.

Another dominant use of the passive (as can be easily noted by scanning pages of this book) is to delete mention of the actor entirely — either because mention of the actor is not especially relevant to the context (e.g., "the passive is used in English" rather than "speakers of English use the passive"), or because the actor is unknown (e.g., "The two sentences were recorded on tape"). It has been reported by linguists (Jespersen, 1924) that between 70 and 94 percent of passive sentences found in surveys of English writings contain no mention of the active subject.[3] The use of passive without actors is thus called for by certain contexts, and it would make little sense to speak of the passive as either more or less complex than a corresponding active in such contexts.

Thus we cannot hope for simple metrics of the difficulty involved in processing sentences on the basis of their syntax, because sentences are not used as purely syntactic entities. They are used as syntactic and semantic and pragmatic entities, serving cognitive, affective, and social functions. Research which relates sentence types to usage context promises to lead to the development of a more refined model of psycholinguistic performance — a model which will take account of both strictly linguistic competence and the realization of that competence in actual settings of human communication.

The research described above has revealed more about performance than it has about transformational grammar, and perhaps this is the most fruitful domain of psycholinguistic research. We already understand a little bit about the role of memory and context in the processing of sentences. We have convinced ourselves that sentences are processed on several levels, and that surface structure is not a sufficient guide to the interpretation of sentences. What lies below surface structure certainly has something to do with grammar as described by linguists, but the details are far from clear (either in linguistics or psycholinguistics). If this brief survey of psycholinguistic research on sentence processing has

---

[3]This form is especially overused in scientific writing, where journal editors demand the omission of first-person statements in order to provide an aura of scientific objectivity to publications. A psychologist, for example, is generally not allowed to say in print, "I tested 50 subjects"; rather, he is compelled to say, "50 subjects were tested" (as if thereby all problems of experimenter bias were lifted!).

whetted your appetite, you can follow the progress of the field by scanning the pages of such journals as the *Journal of Verbal Learning and
Verbal Behavior, Language and Speech,* and *Language and Language
Behavior Abstracts.* I suspect that psycholinguistic research in the seventies will be more complex and will show more linguistic sophistica-
tion than that of the sixties, and that increasing attention will be paid to
semantics and linguistic deep structures. Another area to develop more
fully will be the study of linguistic development in the child—and to
that area we now turn.

3

Language Development in the Child

. . . for I was no longer a speechless infant, but a speaking boy. This I remember; and have since observed how I learned to speak. It was not that my elders taught me words . . . in any set method; but I, longing by cries and broken accents and various motions of my limbs to express my thoughts, that so I might have my will, and yet unable to express all that I willed, or to whom I willed, did myself, by the understanding which Thou, my God, gavest me, practise the sounds in my memory. . . . And thus by constantly hearing words, as they occurred in various sentences, I collected gradually for what they stood; and having broken in my mouth to these signs, I thereby gave utterance to my will. Thus I exchanged with those about me these current signs of our wills, and so launched deeper into the stormy intercourse of human life . . .

—St. Augustine,
Confessions (c. 400 A.D.)

The mystery of how a child learns to speak has intrigued and puzzled adults since antiquity — undoubtedly for millenia before St. Augustine's speculations. The mental abilities of a little child seem to be rather limited in many ways, yet he masters the exceedingly complex structure of his native language in the course of a short three or four years. What is more, each child, exposed to a different sample of the language, and generally with little or no conscious tuition on the part of his parents, arrives at essentially the same grammar in this brief span. That is to say, each child rapidly becomes a full-fledged member of his language community, able to produce and comprehend an endless variety of novel yet meaningful utterances in the language he has mastered.

In Chapter 1 there are passing hints of the implications of modern linguistic theory for our understanding of the tasks of language acquisition. Until recently, behavioristic psychology looked upon language, and the task of first language learning, as just another form of human behavior which could be reduced to the laws of conditioning. The picture we are now beginning to form, however, is that of a child who is creatively constructing his language on his own, in accordance with innate and intrinsic capacities — a child who is developing new theories of the structure of the language, modifying and discarding old theories as he goes. This is a picture which differs radically from the traditional picture of a child whose learning is governed by variables such as frequency, recency, contiguity, and reinforcement. In order to evaluate these theoretical disputes, however, it will first be necessary to examine some of the facts of language acquisition. We will examine the acquisition of syntax in some detail, and will conclude with a brief look at the development of phonology.

The infant's early attempts at vocal communication are quite different from human language in important ways. There is a repertoire of inborn noises expressing a spectrum of need states. However, it will take a long time before vocalizations are used to designate objects or events, to ask and answer questions, and so on. Normally, by the end of the first year the child can produce a number of clearly differentiated sounds, and parents begin to hear what they identify as "first words" coming out of the infant's babblings. These first words often have the force of entire sentences, and have been referred to as "one-word sentences." The meaning of such an utterance varies with the situation, and so "mama" can mean

"Mama come here," or "That's mama," or "I'm hungry," or any number of things. We cannot speak of the child's *active* grammar because he has not yet combined any of his words into longer utterances. It is possible that he already has a "passive" grammatical system; that is, he may be able to understand some grammatical patterns in adult speech, but this delicate and complex research question has not yet been submitted to investigation.

The new picture of child language which I mentioned above has been developed under the impetus of transformational grammar. The methodological implications of this new picture can best be understood by comparing earlier with recent studies of child language. For many long years this was a dreary subfield of developmental psychology consisting of word counts, phoneme counts, counts of sentence types, and the like —all classified on the basis of age. Since the children's words were classed in terms of their part-of-speech membership in adult English, most of these careful and tedious studies (especially tedious since they were carried out before the days of the computer) are impossible to interpret, because the important question is not what part of speech a word is in the adult language, but what role it plays in the child's language system. It seems clear to us now that children form a variety of word categories of their own—based on the functions of words in their own language systems—and so words must be looked at in the light of the *child's* total system, rather than in terms of the adult system, which he has not yet mastered.

The clearest evidence at this time comes from the very earliest stages of language development. Nearly all the work which has been done on the development of grammar so far has focused on the preschool period between about a year-and-a-half and four years of age. A brief examination of the outlines of this work should reveal the relevance of grammatical analysis for an understanding of cognitive development in the child.[1]

GRAMMATICAL DEVELOPMENT

When the child starts putting two words together one can begin investigating his active grammar. The examples presented below demonstrate that child language is structured from this point on, that it soon can be characterized by *hierarchical structures*, that it tends to be *regular*, that the structures change with age, and that they do not always correspond to adult structures.

---

[1] A number of useful reviews of child language acquisition have been prepared recently. The following should be especially helpful to the interested reader: Braine (in press); Brown, Cazden, and Bellugi (1969); Ervin-Tripp, 1966; McNeill (in press). More detailed examination of a number of particular problems can be found in a collection of readings edited by Ferguson and Slobin (in press).

Two-Word Utterances

To begin: One cannot study the child's active grammar until he starts putting two words together to make primitive sentences. This happens typically around eighteen months of age. Several American investigators have dealt with this level (Braine, 1963; Brown and Fraser, 1963; Miller and Ervin, 1964), and since their findings have been remarkably similar, it is possible here to speak in general terms of the typical, two-word-utterance, English-speaking child. The English data correspond remarkably well with what little is known about child language development in a number of other languages (Braine, in press; Slobin, in press a).

The growth of such two-word utterances is at first slow, but rapidly accelerates. For example, the following are figures from the speech of one child (Braine, 1963); the cumulative number of *different* two-word combinations recorded in successive months was 14, 24, 54, 89, 350, 1400, 2500+. It is clear that a huge number of new combinations appeared in a relatively brief span of time.

Distributional analysis reveals that the child does not produce such utterances by mere unstructured juxtaposition of two words; rather, two *classes* of words are revealed by analysis. There is a small class of what have been called "pivot words" by Braine (1963) or "operators" by Miller and Ervin (1964), and a large, open class of words, many of which were previously one-word utterances. For example, a child may say things such as "boot on," "tape on," "fix on," and many other sentences of this type. The word *on* is a sort of "pivot" here—it is always in second position, and a large collection of words can precede it in first position. The child may also say things like "more cookie," "more hot," "more sing," and "more high." In this case one can say that there is a pivot in first position—*more* —which is followed by a large class of words in the child's speech.

On distributional grounds it seems that one of the classes is small and contains words of high frequency in the child's speech. The membership of this class is stable and fairly fixed; these words can be called pivots because other words can be attached to them. A pivot word may be the first or the second member of a two-word sentence—but whichever it is, its position is fixed (at least in English and several other languages). The pivot class expands slowly—that is, only a few pivots enter each month. The other class is large and open, containing all the other words in the vocabulary except the pivots. All of the words in this open class also may occur as single-word utterances; some of the pivots, however, only occur in two-word sentences. Table 1 presents a sample of part of the pivot grammar of a child studied at Harvard (McNeill, 1966). On the left is the total list of first-position pivots (there are nine of them); on the right is a small selection from the open class (which may contain hundreds of

TABLE 1   FRAGMENT OF PIVOT GRAMMAR OF ONE CHILD[1]

$$\left\{\begin{array}{l} \text{allgone} \\ \text{byebye} \\ \text{big} \\ \text{more} \\ \text{pretty} \\ \text{my} \\ \text{see} \\ \text{night-night} \\ \text{hi} \end{array}\right\} \quad \left\{\begin{array}{l} \text{boy} \\ \text{sock} \\ \text{boat} \\ \text{fan} \\ \text{milk} \\ \text{plane} \\ \text{shoe} \\ \text{vitamins} \\ \text{hot} \\ \text{Mommy} \\ \text{Daddy} \\ \bullet \\ \bullet \\ \bullet \end{array}\right\}$$

[1]From McNeill (1966, p. 22).

words at this stage). Generally (with some few exceptions), any word on the left can be combined with any word on the right to form an utterance in this child's language (observing the order rule of left before right).

An important thing to note is that, from the point of view of this analysis of the child's system, he has but two classes of words, though these words belong to a number of different classes according to an analysis of the adult language (e.g., adjectives, nouns, etc.). The main point is that the child already has a system of his own, and it is not a direct copy of the adult system. Already at this stage—and certainly at later stages—many of the child's utterances, although consistent with *his* system, do not directly correspond to the form of adult utterances, and do not look like reduced or delayed imitations of adult utterances. The two-word period is rich with charming examples of such childish utterances (Braine, 1963): "allgone sticky" (after washing hands), "allgone outside" (said when door was shut, apparently meaning, "the outside is all gone"), "more page" (meaning, "don't stop reading"), "more wet," "more car" (meaning, "drive around some more"), "more high" (meaning, "there's more up there"), "there high" (meaning, "it's up there"), "other fix" (meaning, "fix the other one"), "this do" (meaning, "do this"). It is quite unlikely that parents speak to children in this way. What is more likely is that the child is already using the limited linguistic means at his disposal to create novel utterances within his own simple but already structured system. This system, of course, must bear some relation to the speech which he has heard around him, but it is certainly not just a reduced copy of that system.

The pivot analysis, however, is only a description of the *form* of children's utterances. It tells us nothing about the *content* of their speech.

TABLE 2: FUNCTIONS OF TWO-WORD SENTENCES IN CHILD SPEECH, WITH EXAMPLES FROM SEVERAL LANGUAGES[1]

Function of Utterance	LANGUAGE English	German	Russian	Finnish	Luo	Samoan
LOCATE, NAME	there book that car see doggie	buch da [book there] gukuk wauwau [see doggie]	Tosya tam [Tosya there]	tuossa Rina [there Rina] vettä siinä [water there]	en saa [it clock] ma wendo [this visitor]	Keith lea [Keith there]
DEMAND, DESIRE	more milk give candy want gum	mehr milch [more milk] bitte apfel [please apple]	yeshchë moloko [more milk] day chasy [give watch]	anna Rina [give Rina]	miya tamtam [give-me candy] adway cham [I-want food]	mai pepe [give doll] fia moe [want sleep]
NEGATE[2]	no wet no wash not hungry allgone milk	nicht blasen [not blow] kaffee nein [coffee no]	vody net [water no] gus' tyu-tyu [goose gone]	ei susi [not wolf] enää pipi [anymore sore]	beda onge [my-slasher absent]	le 'ai [not eat] uma mea [allgone thing]
DESCRIBE EVENT OR SITUATION[3]	Bambi go mail come hit ball block fall baby highchair	puppe kommt [doll comes] tiktak hängt [clock hangs] sofa sitzen [sofa sit] messer schneiden [cut knife]	mama prua [mama walk] papa bay-bay [papa sleep] korka upala [crust fell] nashla yaichko [found egg] baba kreslo [grandma armchair]	Seppo putoo [Seppo fall] talli 'bm-bm' [garage 'car']	chungu biro [European comes] odhi skul [he-went school] omoyo oduma [she-dries maize]	pa'u pepe [fall doll] tapale 'oe [hit you] tu'u lalo [put down]

TABLE 2 FUNCTIONS OF TWO-WORD SENTENCES IN CHILD SPEECH, WITH EXAMPLES FROM SEVERAL LANGUAGES[1]

Function of Utterance	LANGUAGE					
	English	German	Russian	Finnish	Luo	Samoan
INDICATE POSSESSION	my shoe mama dress	mein ball [my ball] mamas hut [mama's hat]	mami chashka [mama's cup] pup moya [navel my]	täti auto [aunt car]	kom baba [chair father]	lole a'u [candy my] polo 'oe [ball your] paluni mama [balloon mama]
MODIFY, QUALIFY	pretty dress big boat	milch heiss [milk hot] armer wauwau [poor dog]	mama khoroshaya [mama good] papa bol'shoy [papa big]	rikki auto [broken car] torni iso [tower big]	piypiy kech [pepper hot] gwen madichol [chicken black]	fa'ali'i pepe [headstrong baby]
QUESTION[4]	where ball	wo ball [where ball]	gde papa [where papa]	missä pallo [where ball]		fea Punafu [where Punafu]

[1]The examples come from a variety of studies, published and unpublished. Data from the three non-Indo-European languages are drawn from the recent doctoral dissertations of Melissa Bowerman (Harvard, in progress: Finnish), Ben Blount (Berkeley, 1969: Luo), and Keith Kernan (Berkeley, 1969: Samoan). (Luo is spoken here in Kenya.) The examples given here are representative of many more utterances of the same type in each language. The order of the two words in the utterance is generally fixed in all of the languages except Finnish, where both orders can be used freely for some utterance types by some children.

[2]Bloom (1968) has noted three different sorts of negation: (1) nonexistence (e.g. "no wet," meaning "dry"), (2) rejection (e.g. "no wash," meaning "don't wash me"), and (3) denial ("no girl," denying a preceding assertion that a boy was a girl).

[3]Descriptions are of several types: (1) agent + action (e.g. "Bambi go"), (2) action + object (e.g. "hit ball"), (3) agent + object (e.g. "mama bread," meaning "mama is cutting bread"), (4) locative (e.g. "baby highchair," meaning "baby is in the highchair"), (5) instrumental (e.g. "cut knife"), (6) dative (e.g. "throw daddy," meaning "throw it to daddy"). (The use of terminology of grammatical case is suggestive here; cf. Fillmore's (1968) discussion of deep cases as underlying linguistic universals.)

[4]In addition to wh-questions, yes-no questions can be made by pronouncing any two-word sentence with rising intonation, with the exception of Finnish. (Melissa Bowerman reports that the emergence of yes-no questions is, accordingly, exceptionally late in Finnish child language.)

The most recent work on language acquisition has come to pay much more attention to semantic questions, as we begin to search for relations between what a child intends to say and the form of his surface utterance. Pivot constructions, and other early two-word sentences, are able to serve a variety of functions in the child's speech. These are the very basic functions of human language; they are found in the child speech of all cultural groups yet studied, and they are functions which are not, by and large, characteristic of communication systems in other primates. The child is already using language in its most universal and basically human sense at the two-word stage. He spends much of his time naming objects or describing actions. Subject-predicate constructions (which are universal to human language) can be discerned from the start. Both quantitative and qualitative modification appear early on. And there is always some form of negation—a function of human language which I think is particularly important (and for which it may be especially difficult to find analogs in the communication systems of other animals). In short, the language is used to describe the world and to manipulate people. Table 2 presents examples of some of the major functions served by early two-word sentences in child speech in several languages. The cross-linguistic similarities are striking.[2]

In addition to pivot structures, other sorts of two-word sentences begin to develop in child language. (In fact, for some children a distinct pivot stage may not be discernible, or may be very brief.) Early on, it seems clear that the child's system is organized on the two familiar levels —surface and deep. For example, consider the following five examples, all of which seem to be simply *noun + noun* structures on the surface (after Bloom, 1968):

(1) cup glass
(2) party hat

---

[2]There is limited evidence for something like pivot structures in child speech in the following languages: Bulgarian, French, German, Japanese, Luo (Kenya), Russian, Samoan, and Serbian. In all of these languages, with the addition of Finnish as well, there seems to be a small class of frequently used operators and a large, open class of content words. Finnish, however, presents an exception to the fixed positionality of pivots. Melissa Bowerman, in a doctoral dissertation in progress at Harvard, has found the free word order of adult Finnish to be reflected in the two-word utterances of one of her two child subjects (though not in the other). Thus pivot structures need not obey an order rule, although the general distributional characteristics of function words vs. content words seems to be universal. (It might be best, therefore, to replace the term "pivot" by Miller and Ervin-Tripp's term "operator.") Cross-cultural study also reveals that the basic grammatical relations expressed by early child utterances appear to be universal (embodying such basic notions as agent, action, object, locative, etc.). In recent doctoral dissertations at Berkeley, Kernan (1969—studying Samoan child language) and Blount (1969—studying Luo child language) have argued for the insufficiency of pivot analysis, and have demonstrated striking cross-linguistic universals in the early forms and functions of child speech.

(3) Kathryn sock

(4) sweater chair

(5) Kathryn ball

These are not pivot structures. All of these words were members of the open class and could be combined with pivots to serve a demonstrative or ostensive function (e.g., "that cup," "that hat," "hat on," "sock on," etc.). The five sentences, however, seem to express five different sorts of *underlying semantic relationships:*

(1) *conjunction* (e.g., "I see a cup and a glass.")

(2) *attribution* (e.g., "This is a party hat.")

(3) *possession* (e.g., "This is Kathryn's sock.")

(4) *location* (e.g., "The sweater is on the chair.")

(5) *subject-object* (e.g., "Kathryn will throw the ball.")

In the full adult sentences, one can determine the underlying semantic relationships on the basis of their fully developed syntactic form. The meanings of the child's utterances, however, cannot be unequivocally interpreted apart from the context in which they were uttered. Thus the development of syntax makes it possible to speak of things which are not entirely evident in the nonlinguistic situation. The child must be aware of the five semantic relationships expressed above, but he is apparently limited to sentences of two words in length, and cannot express the full relationship in a single utterance. An important aspect of grammatical development, therefore, is the ability to produce longer utterances in which subparts of the utterance bear grammatical relations to one another.

Hierarchical Constructions

As soon as children begin to produce utterances longer than two words, it is clear that their sentences take on a hierarchical structure — that is, it is already possible to analyze sentences in terms of immediate constituents, or structural subunits. Thus the basic organizing principles of language, mentioned in Chapter 1, emerge very early.

The child provides the analyst with striking evidence of the constituent structure of sentences when he expands his own utterances. Often a child will begin with a short sentence, and then fill it in with a longer sentence immediately afterwards. It is as if he first prepared one constituent of a larger sentence, and then "plugged it in" to a more complex sentence. Martin Braine (in press) has noted a number of such "replacement sequences" in two-year-olds. For example, the child may begin with a predicate phrase and then immediately replace it by a subject-predicate construction: "Want that . . . Andrew want that." "Build house . . . Cathy build house." It is clear that these simple three-word sentences are not just strings of three words, but have several layers of constituents. For example, a tree diagram of the last sentence reveals its hierarchical structure:

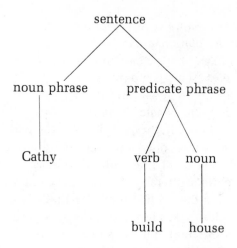

Sometimes the child will go further, and expand the predicate phrase as well: "Stand up . . . Cat stand up . . . Cat stand up|table." In the last utterance, the vertical line indicates an intonation break in the middle of the sentence. The child has clearly analyzed this sentence into its phrase structure constituents of subject ("cat") and predicate ("stand up table"), with the predicate further divided into verb ("stand up") and locative ("table"). Thus the string of words, "Cat stand up table," clearly expresses several basic grammatical relationships.

The child's hesitations also provide evidence of his analysis of sentences into units. For example, Brown and Bellugi (1964) note the following sort of sentence as evidence that noun phrases function as units in the child speech: "Put . . . the red hat . . . on." In this utterance, "the red hat" seems to function as a single unit which can be placed between the two parts of the verb "put on." It is important to note that hesitations do not tend to occur at other locations in such sentences. For example, Brown and Bellugi report the absence of such utterances as "Put the red . . . hat on" or "Put the . . . red hat on." That is, the noun phrase seems to be maintained as an uninterrupted entity.

Sentences, then, are not mere strings of words but hierarchies of units organized according to grammatical principles. The child apparently operates on these basic and universal principles even when composing short, idiosyncratic, childish utterances.

Regularizations

An important point noted above is that child speech deviates from adult speech, and that it deviates in systematic fashion—thus leading one to believe that the deviations are creatively constructed by the child on the basis of a partial analysis of the language and on the basis of inherent cognitive tendencies of the child's mind. The child's creative contribution is clearly revealed in the overregularization of inflections, where consistently deviant utterances appear. Parents and schoolteachers know, for example, that children say things like *comed, breaked, goed, doed,* and so on. That is, the irregular (or "strong") verbs are inflected for past tense as if they were regular (or "weak") verbs. You have probably also heard regularizations of other sorts—say, of the plural, as in *foots, mouses,* and the like. This tendency to regularize continues well into elementary school for some children, and has been noted in a number of languages.

Now, from a traditional psychological point of view, we would expect to find that children begin by using some regular forms correctly—like *walked* and *helped* and so on—and that they extend (or *overextend*) this rule to the irregular verbs. The real story, however, is much more interesting. In all of the cases which have been studied (and these are children of homes where standard English is spoken, and are usually first-born children) the first past tenses used are the correct forms of irregular verbs—*came, broke, went,* and so on. Apparently these irregular verbs in the past tense—which are the most frequent past tense forms in adult speech—are learned as separate vocabulary items at a very early age.

Then, as soon as the child learns only one or two regular past tense forms—like *helped* and *walked*—he immediately replaces the correct irregular past tense forms with their incorrect overgeneralizations from the regular forms. Thus children actually say *it came off, it broke,* and *he did it* before they say *it comed off, it breaked,* and *he doed it.* Even though the correct forms may have been practiced for several months, they are driven out of the child's speech by the overregularization, and may not return for years. This is just one example of a widespread phenomenon, noted by investigators of child speech in many languages (see Braine, in press; Slobin, 1966, in press *a*).

This phenomenon is rather puzzling from the point of view of some approaches to the psychology of learning. The correct irregular forms were already learned, practiced, presumably reinforced. Then suddenly the child begins saying things like *goed*—which could not be imitations, since he has never heard such forms from his parents, and which are certainly not reinforced by his parents. Yet these overgeneralizations persist, sometimes for years. Let me emphasize that this is true of first-born children of intellectual, middle-class homes, who do not hear these incorrect overgeneralizations.

The crucial point here is that the strong verbs, though they are frequent, do not follow a regular pattern, and evidently children are especially sensitive to patterned regularities. As soon as a pattern is noticed, the child will try to apply it as broadly as possible, thus producing words which are regular, even if they have never been heard before. One cannot help but be impressed with the child's great propensity to generalize, to analogize, to look for regularities — in short, to seek and create order in his language.

Another interesting example of regularization comes from the work of Susan Ervin-Tripp and Wick Miller at Berkeley (Miller and Ervin, 1964; Ervine, 1964). Their subjects, like most English-speaking children, regularized the plural of *foot*. Some children would say *foots*; others would say *feets*. At a somewhat later stage, these children learned syllabic plurals, such as *box-boxes*, and replaced the earlier overregularized plural with a new analogic form, *footses*. Or other children, upon learning the pluralization *glass-glasses*, replaced *foots* with *footiz*. Ervin-Tripp concludes that "even highly practiced, familiar plurals may be temporarily changed in form by overgeneralization of new patterns" (Ervin, 1964, p. 177).

Similar phenomena are seen repeatedly in Russian child language, where the abundance of inflections allows for many more overgeneralizations than in English. Again and again a form which has been highly practiced will suddenly be driven out by another, more regular form, and only much later will a proper balance be achieved (see Slobin, 1966, in press *a*; and translations of Soviet studies in Ferguson and Slobin, in press).

Transformations

The development of grammatical transformations is a difficult area to investigate, and the findings are too complex to present in a brief introductory book of this sort (see Braine, in press; McNeill, in press). At the early stage of two-word sentences it is difficult to speak of the presence of transformations. We have noted above that the child's underlying intentions, or meanings, may be more complex than the simple surface utterances he produces. But there is no clear evidence of systematic rules relating underlying meanings to surface utterances. Rather performance factors seem to limit the child to very brief utterances.

There are quite simple procedures for marking such features as interrogation and negation when surface utterances are so brief. A sentence is marked as a question by rising intonation. If the child wants to negate an utterance, he simply attaches *no* or *not*. Because his sentences are so simple, he does not need to use the complex transformational apparatus of adult speech. If our sentences were all short, like "I go," we could make ourselves understood by means of a simple negation: "No I go," or "I go not," or something like that. But if you want to negate a sentence like "He likes girls who carry Greek bags," you can't just put a *no* at the beginning or end and expect to be understood: "No he likes girls who carry Greek bags" or "He likes girls who carry Greek bags no." You have to do some additional work to negate this sentence. If you want to negate the first part, you have to insert *do*, inflect it, and negate it: "He doesn't like girls who carry Greek bags." If you want to negate the second part, you must insert your *do* later, and work on it there: "He likes girls who don't carry Greek bags." (Or you may want to negate both parts.)

So at first the child does not need much of a transformational system because his sentences are short and simple. He can, in fact, get along with sentences like "No sit there" and "Wear mitten no." In the course of his development he has more and more complicated things to say, and must figure out ways of doing so. At first he isn't very good at it, and he invents rather clumsy grammars. Eventually, it seems, these clumsy grammars break down and the child is forced to invent something like a transformational grammar for the sake of efficiency. Ursula Bellugi-Klima has made this point very clear in her analysis of the development of negative and interrogative transformations (Bellugi, 1967), and you might wish to read David McNeill's (1966) lucid summary of this work.

One part of Bellugi-Klima's study (1968) very clearly reveals the existence of separate grammatical transformations in child speech, and we will examine it briefly here. It deals with an aspect of grammar discussed in Chapter 1: the formation of questions with "wh-words" (*what, who, why*, etc.). As mentioned in Chapter 1, children frequently utter questions such as "What the boy hit?" Other typical forms are "What he can ride in?"; "What he wants?"; "Where I should put it?"; and "Why he's doing it?" In all of these examples, the child has correctly performed one grammatical operation—preposing the question word; but he has failed to perform another—inversion of subject and auxiliary. Bellugi-Klima found that at the same stage at which a child produced wh-questions like "What he can ride in?" he also produced inverted yes-no questions like "Can he ride in a truck?" Thus the child was also able to perform the grammatical operation of inversion, or transposing. It seems, therefore, that both preposing and transposing are "psychologically real" operations for the child, for we have evidence that he can perform each of them singly. Apparently there is some performance limitation, some restriction on "sentence programming span," which block the application of both operations together at this stage of development. The child's "error" thus reveals his use of grammatical transformations.

Sentences such as "Where I can put them?" are clearly *produced* by the child. He could not have imitated them from adult speech. Furthermore, when asked to imitate such a sentence a child will often filter it through his own rule system:

> Adult: "Adam, say what I say: Where can I put them?"
> Adam: "Where I can put them?"

It is as if the child even imposes his own structure upon what he hears. Again, as in Chapter 2, we see the phenomenon of an *active* perceiver, processing heard speech according to his own inner structures.

Bellugi-Klima suggests that small children operate under a performance restriction on the number of operations they can perform in generating a sentence. At the stage just discussed, the child is apparently limited to one of the two operations of transposing and preposing, and will fail to transpose in sentences where the adult system requires both operations. At a later stage the sentence programming span apparently increases, and the child is able to perform both operations on one sentence, producing appropriate sentences such as "Why can he go out?" At this stage, however, he cannot produce appropriate adult sentences when three operations are called for. This is clear when the operation of negation is introduced. The negative element must be attached to the auxiliary, and the child demonstrates his control of this operation by producing such sentences as "He can't go out." But note what happens when negation is called for along with preposing and transposing: the child says "Why he can't go out?", failing to transpose, although he transposes correctly in the corresponding affirmative, "Why can he go out?"

Bellugi-Klima demonstrated this phenomenon very clearly with the little boy who is referred to in the literature as Adam. She played a game in which Adam had to ask questions of a puppet shaped like an Old Lady:

> Adult: "Adam, ask the Old Lady where she can find some toys."
> Adam: "Old Lady, where can you find some toys?"
> Adult: "Adam, ask the Old Lady why she can't run."
> Adam: "Old Lady, why you can't run?"

Bellugi-Klima gave numerous problems of this sort to Adam. She concludes: "In his responses, all affirmatives were inverted, all negatives were not. The interpretation again fits with the notion of a limit on the permitted complexity at one stage" (1968, p. 40).

These few examples should make abundantly clear to you the complexity of the task facing a child in the acquisition of his native tongue. Bear these complexities in mind later in this chapter, when we go on to consider the possible psychological bases for such a process of acquisition. First, though, let us consider the notion of "rule" in more detail.

What is a "Rule"?

The discussion so far in this book has made reference repeatedly to the speaker's knowledge of the rules of his language and to the emergence of various sorts of rules in the child. You will remember that I have argued that the great productivity of human language—the ability to produce and understand endless novel sentences—requires that one speak in terms of the formation of grammatical rules, rather than the learning of large numbers of specific word combinations. But this notion of rule is unfortunately slippery, and can be easily misunderstood. The use of this word, *rule*, may lead you to think that psycholinguists believe people can state explicit rules of grammar, and that children learn such rules. This, of course, is not what we have in mind. None of us, for example, can state all of the rules of English grammar. Perhaps this important notion of rule can be clarified by asking about the sorts of behavioral evidence which would enable one to say that a person "possesses" or "acts as if he knew" a rule. (I believe this approach can be fruitfully applied to other realms of social behavior as well, although the discussion here deals with rules in terms of grammatical development in childhood.)

There are various levels of evidence for rules, ranging from weak to stringent. The simplest sort of evidence comes from analysis of natural behavior—in our case the spontaneous speech of the child. For example, at the elementary level of two-word utterances, discussed above, regularities can already be detected, since not all possible word combinations actually occur. This is the earliest sort of evidence for rules ontogenetically—*regularities of behavior.*

A more stringent criterion for the existence of rules is the search for the extension of regularities to new instances. As we have seen, the spontaneous speech of the child can furnish such evidence, as when one encounters utterances such as "it breaked" or "two mouses." Jean Berko (1958) has created an explicit test of children's ability to extend morphological rules to new cases, and her method would be valuable in the developmental study of other rule systems as well. She presents children with new words and invites them to apply their linguistic knowledge to the use of these words. For example, a child is presented with a picture of a little creature called a "wug," and then is asked to name a picture showing two such creatures. If he says "two wugs," one has clear evidence that he knows how to produce this particular English plural ending, since he has clearly never heard the word *wug* before.

But there are even more stringent tests, or definitions, of a rule. Later on in his development, the child will demonstrate a *normative* sense of rules—that is, he will be able to judge if an utterance is correct with respect to some linguistic standard. This is what linguists refer to as a "sense of grammaticality." Several levels of evidence of a sense of grammaticality emerge with age, demonstrating increasing linguistic self-awareness on the part of the child.

Once again, the earliest evidence comes from spontaneous speech. When a child stops and corrects himself one can infer that he is monitoring his speech against some notion of correctness. By age three, self-corrections are frequent. For example, the following was recorded in the free speech of a three-year-old girl: "She had a silly putty like me had . . . like I . . . like I did." It is evident that this girl is checking her speech against her linguistic rules as she goes along. What is equally evident from other utterances is that she is using her *own* rules as the standard for her sense of grammaticality, and not those of adults. For example, later on in the same sample she "corrected" herself as follows: "Why . . . Why . . . Why ducks have not . . . Why ducks have no hands?"

Perhaps a more stringent test of the sense of grammaticality is met when the child detects deviations from the norm in the speech of others. Three-year-olds are also heard to correct the speech of other children (and even of their parents), though the chronological relation between self-correction and correction of others has not been established.

The most stringent criterion of grammatical judgment is response to a direct question. One can ask the child, for example, if it is "better" or "more correct" to say "two foots" or "two feet." This is a major type of data for the linguist working with adult informants. The ability to make such overt grammatical judgments is late to develop in childhood, and, unfortunately, of little use in dealing with very young children. The frustrations resulting from such attempts are aptly captured by the "pop go weasel effect" described by Roger Brown and Ursula Bellugi-Klima (Brown and Bellugi, 1964):

> Interviewer: Now Adam, listen to what I say. Tell me which is better . . . some water or a water.
> Adam (two years old): Pop go weasel.

So far, then, we have the following evidence for rules. We can be fairly sure that a child has some rule system if his production is regular, if he extends these regularities to new instances, and if he can detect deviations from regularity in his own speech and the speech of others. This is generally what psycholinguists mean when they speak of the child's learning, or forming, or possession of linguistic rules. Note that I have left out the most stringent test for the existence of rules, namely: Can the *individual state the explicit rule?* As I pointed out before, using this as evidence, of course, we would all fail the test. Since no complete and adequate grammar of English (or any language) has yet been written, in fact none of us *knows* the rules of English according to this criterion. We can follow them and use them implicitly, but we can state them only rarely, imperfectly, and with uncertainty. Explicit statement of rules is irrelevant to our concerns here and is an entirely different sort of ability than we are considering here. As Susan Ervin-Tripp has put it:

> To qualify as a native speaker . . . one must learn . . . rules. . . . This is to say, of course, that one must learn to behave *as though one knew the rules* [my italics] (Slobin, 1967, p. x).

What this means from the point of view of the scientific observer is that it is possible to describe the speaker's behavior in terms of rules. Such a description, however, should not be taken to imply that the particular rules devised by the scientist are actual entities existing inside the individual in a definite psychological or physiological sense. In very rough and brief form, the sorts of behavior I have just listed constitute evidence for behaving "as though one knew the rules."

Developmental psycholinguists in the United States have collected much evidence of this sort, clearly indicating that at least English-speaking children (both white and black, middle class and lower class) develop, discard, and refine grammatical rule systems, ultimately arriving at adult linguistic competence. Furthermore, the evidence suggests that individual children go though strikingly similar stages of development (see, for example: Brown, Cazden, and Bellugi, 1969; Cazden, 1968; Klima and Bellugi, 1966). What little information we have on children acquiring other native languages suggests a universality of basic stages and processes of acquisition (Braine, in press; Slobin, 1966, in press *a*).

Theories of Language Acquisition

The direction of current theory and research in this field has been to emphasize universality and the existence of innate, biological determinants of such universality (Chomsky, 1968; Lenneberg, 1967). The arguments around the issue of innate factors in language acquisition are complex and heated. The impact of transformational grammar—along with recent work in ethology, perceptual and cognitive development, and other areas—has revived psychologists' interest in nativistic aspects of the growth of intelligence. To many psychologists the postulation of complex, genetically programmed perceptual and cognitive mechanisms is becoming more and more plausible—if not obligatory. The problem of accounting for human language acquisition has long been central in this debate—and it promises to continue to be so.

Theories of language acquisition must also come to terms with the complexity of the task facing the child—especially the problem of discovering *underlying* structures and meanings of sentences. Psychological learning theories are constructed to deal with associations of stimuli and responses, but what the child acquires in the course of language development is not a collection of S-R (stimulus-response) connections, but a complex internal rule system, as discussed above. He is never exposed to the rule system itself, however: he is only exposed to individual sentences in individual situations. How, then, does he acquire the underlying linguistic system on the basis of such evidence?

The complexity of this task has made it plausible (to some) to postulate that the child's mind is somehow "set" in a predetermined way to process the sorts of structures which characterize human language, arriving at something like a transformational grammar of his native language. This is not to say that the grammatical system itself is given as innate knowledge, but that the child has innate means of processing information and forming internal structures, and that, when these capacities are applied to the speech he hears, he succeeds in constructing a grammar of his native language. Indirect evidence for this approach also comes from the fact that there seems to be a biologically-determined "critical stage" for language acquisition in humans (during childhood), and that there are probably special structures in the human brain, lacking in all other animal brains, which perform language functions (Lenneberg, 1967).

These issues are far from settled, and cannot be dealt with here in any extensive way. Perhaps the following quotes from Noam Chomsky will stimulate the reader to follow up the argument in linguistics, philosophy, and psychology.

> . . . knowledge of grammatical structure cannot arise by application of step-by-step inductive operations (segmentation, classification, substitution procedures, filling of slots in frames, association, etc.) of any sort that have yet been developed within linguistics, psychology, or philosophy. . . . It seems plain that language acquisition is based on the child's discovery of what from a formal point of view is a deep and abstract theory—a generative grammar of his language—many of the concepts and principles of which are only remotely related to experience by long and intricate

chains of unconscious quasi-inferential steps. A consideration of the character of the grammar that is acquired, the degenerate quality and narrowly limited extent of the available data, the striking uniformity of the resulting grammars, and their independence of intelligence, motivation, and emotional state, over wide ranges of variation, leave little hope that much of the structure of the language can be learned by an organism initially uninformed as to its general character. . . . (1965, p. 58).

. . . On the basis of the best information now available, it seems reasonable to suppose that a child cannot help constructing a particular kind of transformational grammar to account for the data presented to him, any more than he can control his perception of solid objects or his attention to line and angle. Thus it may well be that the general features of language structure reflect, not so much the course of one's experience, but rather the general character of one's capacity to acquire knowledge — in the traditional sense, one's innate ideas and innate principles (1965, p. 59).

Let us examine some of the major theoretical concepts of psychological learning theory in the light of Chomsky's arguments.[3] A classical approach to acquisition problems such as the one we have been examining is to say that the child is "reinforced" for his performance (both positively and negatively), and that, on the basis of reinforcement, he "generalizes" his future behavior pattern to be closer to that required by the reinforcing agent. Now let us imagine a highly improbable, but theoretically perfect reinforcement situation: every time the child utters a grammatical sentence he receives positive reinforcement, and every ungrammatical sentence receives negative reinforcement. Could this schedule of reinforcement result in grammatical speech? Conceivably it could, but it would tell us nothing of the process whereby the child arrived at the underlying notions of grammar which would make correct performance possible. To find out that a given utterance was in error does not tell the child exactly what he did wrong in producing that utterance, and certainly does not tell him how to correct it the next time (if he ever chooses to utter that particular sentence again). Nor does positive reinforcement give any discriminative information about what was correct about the grammatical construction just uttered. We are still left with the problem of how the child comes to realize the proper relationship between sounds and meanings; how he arrives at the principles of ordering words and parts of words so that they make sense.

For example, suppose a child says "I called up him," and receives

---

[3]Chomsky's (1959) review of Skinner's *Verbal Behavior* presents a forceful and extended exposition of the position against psychological learning theory taken here.

negative reinforcement for an ungrammatical utterance. How does he know what to do next? He has formed this utterance, probably, on analogy with sentences like "I called up Joe," and now has to learn that when the object of a verb-particle construction is a pronoun (like "him") it must always go between the verb and the particle ("I called him up"), while when the object is a noun it can go either between the verb and particle or after the particle. The mere fact that "I called up him" is wrong gives the child no clue as to what is right. Maybe he should have said "I called up he," or "I call-upped him," or any number of other things. The point is that reinforcement could only tell the child that a sentence is globally correct or incorrect. His own cognitive facilities and language acquisition skills are needed in order for him to make use of reinforcement. And it is just these skills and facilities which are the core interest of psycholinguistics.

There are several other important things to say about reinforcement. For one thing, you have seen above (in the discussion of overregularization) that reinforcement could not be a very effective means of shaping language. Certainly, if children receive reinforcement for grammar at all, they receive negative reinforcement for overregularizations of the past tense. Yet these errors are very persistent.

Moreover, parents seem to pay little attention overall to the grammatical correctness or incorrectness of their children's speech. What they are most interested in is what the child has to say, and not the sentence structures he uses. Roger Brown, at Harvard, has been studying three children between the ages of about one and a half and four. Spontaneous interaction between mother and child was recorded weekly over the course of several years. In a recent paper, Brown and his co-workers examined their data to see if mothers are sensitive to the grammaticality of their children's utterances. If they are not, it would be difficult to maintain that child language develops as a result of conscious tuition, or reinforcement, on the part of mothers. Following this argument, Brown looked at cases in which a child's utterance was followed by an expression of approval or disapproval on the part of the adult. There was no evidence that parental responses could play a role in shaping the child's sense of grammaticality. In Brown's cogent summary:

> What circumstances did govern approval and disapproval directed at child utterances by parents? Gross errors of word choice were sometimes corrected, as when Eve said *What the guy idea.* Once in a while an error of pronunciation was noticed and corrected. Most commonly, however, the grounds on which an utterance was approved or disapproved . . . were not strictly linguistic at all. When Eve expressed the opinion that her mother was a

girl by saying *He a girl* mother answered *That's right*. The child's utterance was ungrammatical but mother did not respond to the fact; instead she responded to the truth value of the proposition the child intended to express. In general the parents fit propositions to the child's utterances, however incomplete or distorted the utterances, and then approved or not, according to the correspondence between proposition and reality. Thus *Her curl my hair* was approved because mother was, in fact, curling Eve's hair. However, Sarah's grammatically impeccable *There's the animal farmhouse* was disapproved because the building was a lighthouse and Adam's *Walt Disney comes on, on Tuesday* was disapproved because Walt Disney comes on, on some other day. It seems then, to be truth value rather than syntactic well-formedness that chiefly governs explicit verbal reinforcement by parents. Which renders mildly paradoxical the fact that the usual product of such a training schedule is an adult whose speech is highly grammatical but not notably truthful (Brown, Cazden, and Bellugi, 1967, pp. 57–58).

The notion of "reinforcement" is thus not a very convincing candidate for the explanation of language development. What other notions are available? If you ask the proverbial "man-in-the-street" how children learn to talk, he will hardly think this is a serious question. The typical reply is something like, "They just imitate what they hear." The traditional assumption has been simply that the child acquires new linguistic forms from the speech of his parents through mimicking what they say: he hears something new, repeats it, and so practices the new form. It is only through such practice—it has been thought—that the child's speech can change. For a time the new form is dependent on parental models; later it breaks free.

You have already read a number of arguments against this simple answer. Even in discussing two-word sentences we found that we couldn't account for all of the child's utterances on the basis of reduced imitations of adult speech, because strange combinations occur. Furthermore, Bellugi-Klima's examples of imitation suggest that the child cannot imitate structures which he is not yet capable of producing on his own. Other evidence also supports this observation (Ervin, 1964; Slobin and Welsh, in press). Besides, even if a child could successfully imitate all of the utterances he hears, we would not understand how he goes on to produce new utterances which he has not heard before.

An even stronger argument against the necessity of imitation for language acquisition is the fact that children who cannot speak at all, but who can hear normally, acquire normal linguistic competence—as far as comprehension is concerned. Eric Lenneberg (1962) has reported a case of a boy who was unable to articulate speech, yet learned to understand the complexities of English utterances. Obviously, the same linguistic competence must underlie both the production and interpretation of speech. Surely it is clear that a speechless child could never have imitated speech, nor have been reinforced for speaking—yet these handicaps did not interfere with his acquisition of linguistic competence.

Perhaps one reason why psychologists have relied on factors like reinforcement and imitation in attempting to account for language acquisition is that they do not realize the complexity of the grammar developed by the child, and have not adequately assessed the nature of the speech heard by the child. One of the motivations for postulating innate mechanisms in language acquisition is the notion that the speech input is not a rich enough source for the induction of grammar. That is, as pointed out repeatedly above, the surface structures of sentences do not provide sufficient information for the interpretation of those sentences.

Some learning theorists, however, postulate a simple input which supports a simple grammar. The simplest syntactic model is a Markov process, as discussed in Chapter 1. Accordingly, the simplest model of language acquisition is to assume that the child hears strings generated by such a left-to-right grammar, learns the transitional probabilities between words, and speaks an associative chain language. For example, Arthur and Carolyn Staats propose:

> It would seem that certain word responses come to follow other word responses because in the spoken and written customs of a language community those words as stimuli occur in that order. A suggested mechanism is that verbal behavior which parallels these customs is reinforced; behavior which does not is not reinforced (Staats and Staats, 1963, p. 169).

The reader who has assimilated the psycholinguistic model presented in this book thus far should be able to evaluate this theory of language acquisition on his own.

Slightly more complex learning models of language acquisition have based themselves on phrase structure grammars in which sentences are held to consist of sequences of word classes (e.g., article-noun-verb, and so forth). In such models (e.g., Jenkins and Palermo, 1964) it is held that the child learns word classes like noun and verb, and the positions in which such classes can occur in sentences. According to such a model, for example, a child should learn that words like boy and dog are members of the same class because they can follow the. This approach, of course, says nothing about how children arrive at the underlying meanings of sentences. However, even as a model of the learning of word classes it faces serious difficulties. Imagine, for example, learning the privileges of occurrence of the word *dog* on the basis of even the following very limited speech input: "Look at the *dog*. The *dog* is here. The *dog* is furry. This is my *dog*. This is my big *dog*. That's no *dog*. Don't kick Jimmy's *dog*. Put the hat on the *dog*. He was bitten by a *dog*. Whose *dog* bit him? Was it your *dog* that got lost?" It is clear that sentences are not simply sequences of words; nor are they simply sequences of word classes.

The rules which a child must develop deal with underlying grammatical structures and the ways in which these structures are reflected in surface utterances. Psychological theories which deal just with characteristics of the surface utterances are not equipped to deal with the essential facts of language processing. We do not yet have an adequate theory of language acquisition. However, as Chomsky has pointed out in the lengthy quotation earlier in this chapter, the traditional approaches of psychological theory do not seem to offer much hope in dealing with this large and complex problem.

Much more remains to be said about the important debate between learning theory and cognitive psychology on the roles of innate and acquired factors in language development. A forthcoming book (Slobin, in press *b*) presents a range of theoretical arguments on all sides. These arguments, and the relevant data, are also lucidly reviewed by McNeill in a valuable review article (1970). A major point for the introductory reader to remember is that a study of language acquisition has posed crucial challenges to much of traditional psychological theorizing about the nature of human development. While the issues have yet to be adequately solved, it is certain that psychology will not emerge unchanged from the coming years of debate and research. What is bound to emerge will be a more complex image of the psychological nature of man, involving complex internal mental structures, in part genetically determined, in part determined by the subtlety and richness of the environment provided by human culture, and probably only minimally determined by traditional sorts of reinforced stimulus-response connections.

PHONOLOGICAL DEVELOPMENT

Questions of phonology do not receive full treatment in this short book. However, some of the fundamental issues of both phonology and development can be illuminated by a brief consideration of the child's acquisition of the sound structure of his language.

Phonology is a complex field, which overlaps with physics when problems of *acoustic phonetics* are raised, and which overlaps with physiology and anatomy when problems of *articulatory* or *motor phonet-ics* are raised. There is no clear agreement among linguists today as to the exact structure of phonological systems — or even as to all of the underlying principles (e.g., compare Gleason, 1961, with Chomsky and Halle, 1968). Rather than elaborate a particular phonological theory here, I will discuss some general psycholinguistic questions in the light of the child's acquisition of phonology — that is, his developing ability to perceive differences between speech sounds and to use such differences in communicating linguistically.

You probably know that there are classes of sounds in language, partially represented by the letters of the alphabet. Perhaps you have heard the term "phoneme," which is one way of referring to such sound classes. If you think for a moment, you will realize that the classes of sounds do not correspond directly to the letters of the alphabet. For example, both *c* and *k* can represent the same sound in some cases (e.g., the initial sounds in *carrot* and *karat*), but *c* can also represent an *s*-sound (as in *recess*). Other sounds require two letters to be represented, as *sh* and *ch*. But, imperfect as it is, the writing system is based on the possibility of representing classes of sounds by a single symbol.

These classes of sounds, sometimes called phonemes, seem to be "psychologically real" to speakers of a language, although there are distinguishable acoustic differences between members of a class. Let me give you a dramatic example to make this concept clear. You probably think that the letter *p* represents a single sound in English. Most English-speaking people hear the *p* in *pin* and the *p* in *spin* as identical, and have no trouble learning to use the same letter to represent these two sounds. But there is a simple experiment you can perform to convince yourself that they really are very different. Hold a lighted match in front of your lips and say *spin*: nothing much will happen to the flame. But now say *pin*: the match is blown out! When you say *pin* there is a strong puff of air following the *p*. That puff is aspiration. In English, aspiration occurs with *p*, *t*, and *k* (voiceless stops) when they occur at the beginning of a word, but aspiration does not occur with these sounds in English when they are part of an initial consonant cluster.

This example demonstrates that classes of sounds in a given language are distinguished by certain *distinctive features*, such as aspiration. Other distinctive features have to do with whether a sound is a vowel or a consonant, whether it is produced with or without vibration of the vocal cords, whether it is a continuous sound or a single puff of air, and so on. These distinctive features, explored at length by the linguist Roman Jakobson (Jakobson and Halle, 1956), are apparently linguistic universals. That is, there is a small set of distinctions used by all languages, probably as a consequence of the anatomical structure of the human articulatory apparatus and the associated brain formations. What the child has to learn is what phonological features are used in his particular language, and how they are used to make contrasts between sounds.

It is important to note that different languages use phonological features in different ways. For example, in Hindi aspiration is used to distinguish between sounds at the beginning of words, so that in Hindi a word like the English *pin* could be pronounced two different ways, with and without initial aspiration, and could have two different meanings, just as *pin* and *bin* have two different meanings in English. Differences between languages are not in terms of sounds which are "harder" or "easier" to pronounce. It is merely the fact that languages use the universal collection of distinctive features to set up different categories of sounds.

In comparing aspiration in Hindi and English, Hindi makes more distinctions than we do. In other regards, English makes more distinctions than some other languages. Consider, for example, the contrast between the voiced consonent *s* and the voiceless *z*. The Spanish speaker often has trouble in learning to distinguish the English pronunciation of these two sounds because they are members of the same class in his language. Spanish makes use of both sounds, as does English, but their occurrence is determined by the other sounds in the word. As a consequence, *rise* and *rice*, or *ice* and *eyes* may be practically indistinguishable for the Spanish speaker. Apparently people learn to make sharp perceptual distinctions between acoustic cues only when those cues play a systematic role in the phonological structure of their language (see Liberman et al., 1967). Again, as pointed out above in regard to grammar, the human perceiver of linguistic messages is not a passive tape recorder. Rather, he imposes his own internal structures upon the acoustic messages he receives.

How might such structures develop in childhood? The notion of distinctive features is very useful here (see Brown, 1965, pp. 196–205; Jakobson, 1968). Apparently the child begins with a simple and global distinction between vowels and consonants, not attending to differences between sounds within those two classes. With development, these classes are divided and re-divided as new contrasts enter the system. All along, the child uses the universal principle of distinguishing classes of sounds by distinctive features, but it takes several years for him to arrive at the full complement of features employed distinctively by his native language.

For example, let us discuss the feature of *voicing*. All consonants can be produced with or without vibration of the vocal cords. Compare these pairs of sounds: *b-p, d-t, g-k, z-s*. In each pair, the position of the tongue and teeth is the same; the only difference is that the vocal cords vibrate when you pronounce the first member of a pair, and do not vibrate when you pronounce the second. The reader should be able to find all of the other pairs of voiced and voiceless consonants in English.

Now, in studying a particular language (either a foreign language or the language of a child), you want to know how distinctive features are used to *contrast* sounds. In the example given above of *bin* and *pin*, you now see that these two words are identical except for the presence or absence of voicing on the first consonant. This is evidence that voicing is used as a distinctive feature in English. Suppose that a child had the voiced *b* only at the beginning of words and the voiceless *p* only at the end; there would be no way of determining if the two sounds were used contrastively. Hence there would be no way of determining if voicing was yet a distinctive feature for this child. The child might use the word *ba* to mean both "ball" and "pie," and the word *gup* to mean both "cub" and "cup." This should remind you of the discussion of early grammar; in analyzing child speech you must look to see what role is played by certain sounds or certain words *in his system*. The presence of an element does not mean that it necessarily belongs to the same category as it does in adult speech. Thus, in the case of pivot sentences, although there were words classed as nouns and adjectives and verbs in adult speech, we could not yet attribute these classes to the child; and in the example above, although the sounds of *p* and *b* are present, we cannot yet attribute the underlying distinctive feature of voicing to the child, because he does not use it to distinguish between words having different meanings.

Here is an actual example of a special system in the phonology of a child. These are some selections of pronunciations in the speech of a linguist's daughter (Velten, 1943):

Adult word	Child's pronunciation
bad	bat
cut	dat
cup	dap
lamb	bap

Note that she does not contrast voiced and voiceless sounds: the voiced sounds *b* and *d* are used only at the beginning of words; the voiceless *p* and *t* at the end. This means that the child has only two consonant classes ("consonant phonemes") at this stage: *b-d* and *p-t*, whereas in adult English these are four classes. Later, voicing became a contrastive feature, allowing the child to double her stock of consonant classes. It is interesting to discover that distinctive features enter a child's speech systematically. When this girl learned to contrast *p* and *b*, she also learned to contrast *t* and *d*, and also *s* and *z*. That is, she learned to apply the contrasting feature of voiced-voiceless to a number of relevant sound classes at once. Again, we are struck by the attempts by the child to organize his speech system. He does not advance by parrot-like imitation, or by gradual learning. Rather, he seizes upon general principles and applies them to many parts of his linguistic system. And, once again, the insights of modern linguistics help us to understand the sort of organization developed by the child.

As in the discussion of acquisition of syntax, learning theory notions seem to be of little relevance. Again, reinforcement could not inform the child as to how to change his utterances to correspond with adult pronunciation. Certainly there is nothing in reinforcement which would determine the fact that the child goes through a series of successive stages, applying more and more contrasting distinctive features to his phonological system before arriving at the full adult system.

In the case of phonology, it is clear that the child does not even have to be able to produce sounds in order to perceive the relevant contrasts. For example, a linguist reports the following dialogue (Miller, 1963):

> Recently a three year old child told me her name was Litha. I answered "Litha?" "No, *Litha*." "Oh, Lisa." "Yes, Litha."

Clearly this child attended to the contrast between English *s* and *th*. She rejected an adult imitation of her pronunciation, even though she was not yet able to produce the contrast herself.

Again, Eric Lenneberg's case study of a speechless child (1962) presents the most conclusive evidence against postulating imitation and reinforcement for speaking as relevant unavoidably necessary variables in language acquisition. You will recall that this child was unable to produce normal, articulated speech. Yet he was perfectly able to understand all of the major complexities of English phonology and syntax. He could understand stories and answer questions about them by pointing to pictures or nodding his head, he could carry out complicated instructions, and so on. Studies of such children ("anarthric children") have demonstrated that their perception of phonological contrasts is normal. Yet these children have never imitated speech and have never been reinforced for saying anything. Clearly, the human mind is capable of refined information processing and analysis, resulting in a total linguistic system. As yet, we have a very limited understanding of the psychological and physiological mechanisms underlying these achievements. The coming years of research in developmental psycholinguistics promise to be exciting ones.

4

Problems of Meaning

When, however, the problem [of the meaning of mean-
ing] is scientifically approached, we find that no less
than sixteen groups of definitions [of meaning] can
be profitably distinguished . . .

—C. K. Ogden and I. A. Richards,
The Meaning of Meaning (1923)

"That's a great deal to make one word mean,"
Alice said in a thoughtful tone.
"When I make a word do a lot of work like that,"
said Humpty Dumpty, "I always pay it extra."
"Oh!" said Alice. She was too much puzzled to
make any other remark.

—Lewis Carroll,
Through the Looking Glass (1872)

When one considers the centuries of writing and research on myriad aspects of "meaning," perhaps an Alice-like response is most appropriate. Meaning is one of the most ambiguous and controversial terms in the theory of language. Meaning permeates so much of our language use that it is difficult to find its borders. Linguistic meaning allows us to evaluate the truth values of sentences, to make paraphrases, to interpret and laugh at anomalies, to understand ambiguities, and to agree on the appropriateness of figurative usage. In childhood we learn how to use words in relation to situations and in relation to each other. Much of our adult learning, talk, and dispute revolves around questions of the proper meaning of words and utterances. Where can one begin to take hold of this network of problems?

Psycholinguistic approaches to the problem of linguistic meaning can be divided into (1) *structural approaches,* which specify dimensions and attributes of meaning, and (2) *process approaches,* which are concerned with the acquisition and comprehension of linguistic meaning. People who are interested in the structures which underlie meanings include dictionary makers, philologists, and certain linguists, philosophers, psychologists, and anthropologists. These people are interested in the dimensions and categories of meaning, the definitions of words, the manner in which combinations of words gain meaning in sentences, and so on. Implicitly, of course, these are the things which a child must learn in order to speak appropriate and meaningful utterances. But one can concern himself with these questions of analysis and structure without deciding how language is learned, or what happens in the head when we intend to speak or when we comprehend the utterances of others. The first part of this chapter deals with several attempts to analyze the structure of meaning. In the second part of the chapter we will be concerned with some theories of the psychological processes underlying the meaningful use of language. The small collection of theories of structure and process briefly presented here makes no claim to be exhaustive. Further discussion can be found in Brown (1958), Fodor and Katz (1964), Osgood et al. (1957), and in the references cited in the course of the discussion.

You will recall from Chapter 1 that the model of generative grammar includes a semantic component which functions as an *interpretive* element; that is, it receives deep structures as input, and its output consists of semantic interpretations. As mentioned earlier, this aspect of grammar is in great ferment at present, and there is no generally accepted model of the relation of syntactic structures to semantic interpretations. In all theories, however, somewhere in the base component of grammar there is a lexicon, or dictionary of meaningful elements in the language. Our concern here is with the lexicon and its structure. Essentially, all of the problems discussed in the first part of the chapter deal with the structure of the lexicon. The problem is one of finding the *semantic features* of items in the lexicon. This problem is, in many ways, similar to the problem of finding distinctive features in phonology. The task is to find the basic units of meaning—both universal and specific to given languages.

STRUCTURAL APPROACHES TO MEANING

Word Meaning

Though the division is by no means clear-cut, we can roughly divide the discussion of structural approaches to meaning into questions of the meanings of words and their components, and questions of the meanings of combinations of words in sentences. Strictly speaking, the "word" is not a unit of linguistic analysis, because a word can be made up of one meaningful unit (e.g., "swim"), or two (e.g., "swimmer"), or three (e.g., "swimmers"), and so on. That is, there are prefixes and suffixes which themselves carry meaning. For our general purposes here, however, we will think of words as minimal units of meaning (cf. the classical linguistic notion of "morpheme"), ignoring the thorny linguistic issues connected with this simplification. In addition, we had best limit ourselves to "content words" (mainly nouns), omitting "function words" (like articles and prepositions), whose role is that of performing syntactic functions rather than carrying explicit meanings in the sense discussed here.

The problem at issue is that of analyzing the *denotative* meanings of words. Crudely put: Can the world of objects and experience to which language refers be broken down into a collection of attributes or dimensions which can characterize all of the words of human language? Among the investigators who have dared to tackle some of the serious problems of denotative meaning have been anthropologists who have been forced to figure out such problems by the necessities of field work with strange peoples speaking strange tongues. From this work has evolved a provocative research technique and body of literature dealing with "componential analysis" (cf. papers and references in Gladwin and Sturtevant, 1962; Hymes, 1964; and Romney and D'Andrade, 1964b).

Componential Analysis   The main evidence we have on the feasibility of analyzing word meanings into semantic components comes from work on kinship terminology of various peoples, and, more recently, on the analysis of terminology in various domains of "ethnoscience," embracing the folk taxonomies of botany, disease, zoology, and the like. The attempt is to find a few underlying dimensions—reminiscent of distinctive features in phonology—upon which all of the kinship terms (or plant terms, or disease names, or what) of a cultural group can be placed.

Let us examine componential analysis using a semantic area with which you have some familiarity: the American kinship system. The task is to discover the semantic *components* which distinguish between the meanings of English kin terms. The anthropologists who have done this work—Wallace, Goodenough, Atkins, and others—have isolated three dimensions which can be used for classifying all of the kinship terms used in America for referring to "blood relatives."

In order to carry out this sort of analysis we must begin by listing all of the kin terms used in the society we are studying. (In our case it is fairly simple, but with a little thought you can imagine the field problems involved in eliciting a set of terms from native informants.) Let's limit ourselves to two generations up and two generations down, and ignore the distinctions between "numbered" cousins (first, second, once removed, etc.) and the distinctions introduced by the modifiers *great* (as in *great aunt*) and *grand* (as in *grand niece*) when used as separate words. This gives us the following terms: *father, mother, grandfather, grandmother, son, daughter, grandson, granddaughter, uncle, aunt, nephew, niece, brother, sister,* and *cousin.* Wallace and Atkins (1960) note that, with the exception of *cousin*, all of these terms indicate the sex of the relative. Some of the terms indicate generation. All of the terms indicate whether the relative is in the "same line" as the speaker: some ("lineals") are either ancestors or descendants in a direct line of descent; others ("nonlineals") share ancestors with the speaker, but are not themselves ancestors or descendants of the speaker. Nonlineals can be further divided into two categories of relatives. In the case of some nonlineal relatives ("colineals") all of the ancestors of the speaker are also ancestors of the relative; in the case of other nonlineal relatives ("ab-lineals") only some of the speaker's ancestors are also ancestors of the relative.

These observations led Wallace and Atkins to hypothesize the following three dimensions as sufficient to define all of the kin terms in question:

A. Sex of the relative (male = a_1, female = a_2)
B. *Generation* of the relative (two generations above ego = $b + 2$, one generation above ego = $b + 1$, ego's generation = 0, one generation below ego = $b - 1$, etc.).

C. *Linearity*: lineal = c_1 (includes ancestors or descendants of ego), colineal = c_2 (nonlineals, all of whose ancestors include, or are included in, all the ancestors of ego), ab-lineal = c_3 (blood relatives neither lineal nor colineal).

The matrix of these three dimensions can be represented in the following diagram:

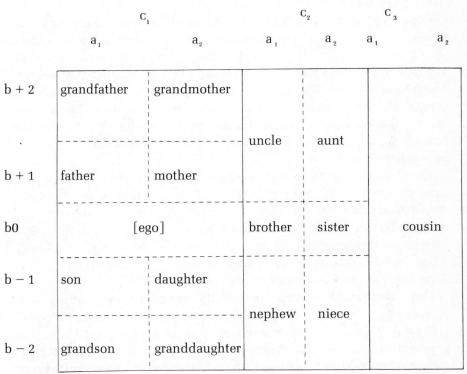

	c_1		c_2		c_3	
	a_1	a_2	a_1	a_2	a_1	a_2
b + 2	grandfather	grandmother				
			uncle	aunt		
b + 1	father	mother				
b0	[ego]		brother	sister	cousin	
b − 1	son	daughter				
			nephew	niece		
b − 2	grandson	granddaughter				

Reproduced by permission of the American Anthropological Association from *American Anthropologist*, Vol. 62, No. 1, 1960.

Wallace and Atkins say about this diagram: "Evidently each term has been so defined, with respect to the components selected, that no term overlaps or includes another; every component is discriminated by at least one term; and all terms can be displayed on the same paradigm. We do not wish to argue that this is the best representation; only that it is adequate to define the set of terms chosen" (p. 62).

We shall return to this last point in a moment. But first let me point out how a componential analysis of this sort could be usefully employed in contrasting the American kinship system with kinship systems in other languages. For example, German makes a sex distinction (a_1-a_2 in regard to cousins, having terms for a male cousin (*Kusin*) and a female cousin (*Kusine*), where we make no distinction. The German system is thus clearly not very far from our own: we do not have to add a new component; merely extend the application of an English component (sex) to another dimension (ab-lineality) which is already used in our system. Contrast the German example with the Turkish kin term *abla,* "older sister." We have no way of fitting this into the English diagram, because we have no component for age (only generation). In order to fit the Turkish term into such a diagram, we would have to add a new semantic component, "older than ego."

Componential analysis is thus a very useful method for getting at the underlying, distinctive semantic features of a given collection of terms. But there are two central problems of this sort of analysis. One problem is whether such an analysis of a domain, like that of kinship presented above, has any psychological reality—if it reflects anything about the way in which we actually think of kinship terms. The other, larger problem is whether this technique of componential analysis can be applied to other sorts of domains than kinship. First let us take up the question of psychological reality.

This is an important question, because many anthropologists hope that they are representing the cognitive structures existing in the minds of speakers, and not just inventing convenient summary systems of terminologies for their own benefit. And clearly this is the psycholinguist's interest in componential analysis. The question is most clearly posed when we have *alternative* componential analyses for a given domain. Is there any good way to choose between alternatives?

This question has been insightfully examined by Romney and D'Andrade, in an article called "Cognitive aspects of English kin terms" (1964a). In this paper they demonstrate that the Wallace and Atkins diagram which you have just examined is not the only possible one for English kin terms. They propose an alternative analysis. In their system, co-lineal and ab-lineal are collapsed into one category called "collateral," which is opposed to "direct." Sex and generation are still relevant components. And there is a new component called "reciprocity." This applies to pairs of terms like *father-son, uncle-niece,* and so on; you can see why they are called reciprocal. Using these components, Romney and D'Andrade come up with the following diagram.

In regard to this diagram, Romney and D'Andrade point out: "Note that the dotted lines represent the relations between terms obtained with simple operations on the notation scheme. [This is in reference to their procedure for establishing the diagram.] Since the notation scheme represents the genealogical elements, it may be assumed that terms joined by dotted lines are somehow 'closer' than terms separated by solid lines. (Although Wallace and Atkins use dotted lines between sex pairs, e.g., mother and father, they are not derived from steps in the analysis.) The

	Direct		Collateral		
	male	female	male	female	
+2	grandfather	grandmother	uncle	aunt	+
−2	grandson	granddaughter			
+1	father	mother	nephew	niece	−
−1	son	daughter			
0	brother	sister	cousin		0

Reproduced by permission of the American Anthropological Association from *American Anthropologist*, Vol. 66, No. 3, 1964.

dotted lines arise from the analytic procedures" (p. 153). The exact details of the procedures are not crucial here; what is important to our discussion is that Romney and D'Andrade provide a measure which predicts which terms should be psychologically "closer" to one another.

Now, given two analyses—that of Wallace and Atkins, and that of Romney and D'Andrade—how can one decide which of these systems is the one which we really "carry around with us in our heads": is it one of the two, neither, or both? It is possible that different Americans use different structures, or that an individual American uses several structures for different purposes. Romney and D'Andrade say:

> It is our feeling that there will usually be several alternative analyses possible for any set of kin terms. If we are to talk about psychological or cognitive implications of an analysis, we must specify what these implications might be. Probably some analyses will be more useful for some purposes and less useful for others. Thus there may be no single best solution for a given system p. 154).

Romney and D'Andrade offer a number of comparisons of the two analytic systems. For one thing, you will notice that their solution stresses the distinction between relatives in the nuclear family (father-mother-son-daughter) and those outside the nuclear family. Since this seems like a "natural unit," and it is ignored in the Wallace and Atkins scheme, perhaps Romney and D'Andrade have hit upon a better way of characterizing the semantic structure of our kin terms.

But these two investigators did not draw conclusions on impressionistic evidence alone; they looked for behavioral evidence of the psychological reality of systems of componential analysis. Using large samples of American high-school students, they carried out a series of ingenious experiments. I'll briefly summarize a few of them here; you can find them described in detail in the original study. The general prediction which Romney and D'Andrade made "from componential analyses to cognitive measures is that the more components any two terms have in common, the greater will be the similarity of response to these terms. The prediction is derived from the assumption that the components of a term constitute the meaning of that term for an individual; hence, the more components which are shared, the more similar the meaning" (p. 154).

First of all they had 105 high-school students "list all the names for kinds of relatives and family members" they could think of in English. They found, of course, that some terms were more "salient" than others—that is, they were listed more frequently, and earlier in the lists. The most salient terms for high-school students were *father* and *mother*. They also found, interestingly enough, that *son* and *daughter* are low in saliency for high-school students: less than a third of them remembered to include these terms. So the cognitive structures you have of a domain like kinship seem to depend in part on what age you are. Romney and D'Andrade also found their component of "reciprocity" a useful one: reciprocal pairs like *father-mother* and *uncle-aunt* were almost always listed together.

The data also supported the linking of terms in their analytical scheme. Groups of terms which could be modified in the same way —by modifiers like *step, in-law, great, half, second*—were also groups which hang together in the diagram. None of the groupings in the diagram are partitioned by any modifying word—i.e., any area within solid lines includes a set of terms all of which can take the same modifier (e:g., *great* can be applied to all terms in the upper left-hand corner, *half* can be applied to both terms in the lower left hand corner, and so on). This is taken as evidence that sets of terms occurring with the same modifier are bound together by components, and that, therefore, the terms themselves are probably classified by speakers on the basis of these components.

Romney and D'Andrade also gave their subjects a series of triad tests, presenting them with three kin terms at a time, and asking them which one was least like the other two. They always found that terms which differed by only one component were classed together, and those differing by more than one were not. For example, consider the subset of kin terms in the nuclear family. We are dealing with only two components here — sex and generation. *Father* and *mother* are the same generation, but differ in regard to the component of sex. *Father* and *son* have the same sex component, but differ on the generation component. And *father* and *daughter* do not share either of these two components (though they do share other components). Presenting all possible triads for this set of four kin terms, Romney and D'Andrade predicted that

> the term *father* will be classed as more similar to *mother* than to *daughter* and classed as more similar to *son* than to *daughter*. This will hold true no matter what strength is given to the component of sex compared to the component of generation. That is, even if a person regards sex differences as trivial and generation differences as extreme, so long as some strength is given to sex differences, *father* will be classed as more similar to *son* than to *daughter* (p. 162).

The following diagram shows the pairings of all four kin terms, presented in all four possible triads. The numbers in parentheses represent the mean number of times a pair of terms was classed together (thus the higher the number the closer the terms in some sort of "cognitive space").

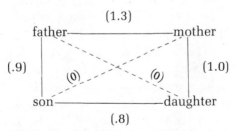

Reproduced by permission of the American Anthropological Association from *American Anthropologist*, Vol. 66, No. 3, 1964.

Thus the data match the prediction. No subject crossed two components in classing a pair of kin terms together. In more complicated triad tests, Romney and D'Andrade found that their predictions of relations between terms were more successful than predictions made on the basis of the Wallace and Atkins scheme. They conclude that it is useful to consider "that the components isolated by a formal analysis define the meaning of a term," and that "one of the componential analyses fits the data better than the other. . . . A major conclusion of this paper is that people respond to kinship terms as if each term contained a bundle of distinct meanings."

This discussion should have given you some idea of the method and implications of componential analysis. Studies such as these represent some of the most detailed attempts to describe the structure of semantic domains, and are of great significance not only to anthropology, but to linguistics and cognitive psychology as well. However, a crucial question in regard to this method is that of the range of its applicability. What other domains are susceptible to this sort of analysis? There have been successful analyses of domains such as plant and animal taxonomies, but the range of possibilities seems to be limited. The analysis seems to work best when dealing with discretely different referent classes. For example, a person is either male or female, either sibling or not, and so on. Each of these terms has a clearly distinguishable, objectively definable referent. It may also be possible to apply componential analysis to more elusive domains, like social relations. For example, what is the distinction between the verbs *give* and *bestow*? It seems that one bestows when giving to social inferiors. Perhaps, then, it can be said that "status" is a component, or distinctive feature of certain verbs (as it is of second-person pronouns in languages which make the "polite-familiar" distinction, such as the *tu-vous* of French, the *du-Sie* of German, etc.).

What sorts of domains seem to present difficulties to compential analysis? Take the word *chair* as an example. It seems to refer to a class which shades off at its boundaries in all directions. When the back of a *chair* gets low enough, or its legs get long enough, it becomes a *stool*; when the seat gets wide enough, it becomes a *bench*, and so on. But there is no way in which an uncle can shade off into an aunt. Rather than having discrete components underlying the meaning of *chair*, then, we seem to be dealing with the intersection of a variety of *dimensions* —and these dimensions are very difficult to specify.

The terms *friend* and *acquaintance* constitute another set in which the distinction seems to be in terms of degree, rather than presence or absence of a given component. A. Richard Diebold (unpublished) has diagrammed these English terms on the basis of relative "social distance" between ego (the speaker) and various alters. Those within the inner circle we call *friends*; those in the outer circle, *acquaintances*. The relative length of the line connecting ego to various alters (small circles) represents social distance. The diagrams for American English and for German are identical except for the location of the inner circle, which is the boundary between the two concepts. That is, we are dealing in both cases with a speaker ("ego") and a collection of specific people standing at given social distances from him.

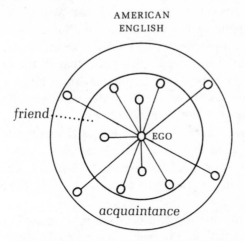

Compare the English terms to their German equivalents, *Freund* and *Bekannter* (or, in the feminine, *Bekannte*). The German terms translate as *friend* and *acquaintance*, respectively, but differ in terms of usage, according to Diebold. The following diagram shows that Germans restrict usage of *Freund* to closer "friends" than we do; that is, many of the people we refer to as friends would count only as acquaintances in German. Note that the two arrays of actual people represented in the American and German diagrams are identical; but the definitions of the terms are different. It is hard to specify a semantic "component" which distinguishes between the American *friend* and the German *Freund*. Again, the distinguishing attribute seems to be one of degree, or position along some dimension.

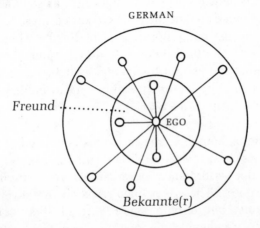

It seems clear from a variety of semantic analyses that the notion of semantic components, or semantic primes, is a useful one. We are still a long way from adequately characterizing a set of semantic universals, but it already seems certain that some of them will be discrete categories, like the components revealed in componential analysis. Some of them will probably be dimensions (like status, social distance, hue, and so on). It is not at all clear to me at this point that all the semantic information about a word can be stated in plus-or-minus terms — i.e., presence or absence of a given feature, as in distinctive feature analysis in phonology. This is, however, the hope on which some semantic theories are currently being constructed. Componential analysis, together with numerous methods developed by field anthropologists for eliciting terms and grouping them (in terms of categories, hierarchies, contrast sets, etc.), can make important contributions to understanding the nature of semantic structure.

At the same time another approach, from the time-honored domain of associationist psychology, is beginning to make contributions to the problems of denotative meaning. I am referring to psycholinguistic analyses of word association data, which we shall turn to next.

Word Associations.   The word association test is one of the oldest tools of experimental psychology. George Miller vividly describes the invention of this technique:

> Sir Francis Galton (1879), English scientist and cousin of Charles Darwin, was the first to try the word-association experiment. He wrote each of 75 different words on a separate card and filed the cards away for several days. Then he looked at the cards one at a time. He timed himself with a stop-watch, starting at the moment the word caught his eye and stopping it as soon as the word had suggested two different ideas. He recorded these ideas as he went through the list but refused to print them. "They lay bare," he commented, "the foundations of a man's thoughts with a curious distinctness, and exhibit his mental anatomy with more vividness and truth than he would probably care to publish to the world" (Miller, 1951, pp. 175–176).

Since then the technique has been extensively used by psychologists and psychiatrists to probe individual minds, to establish laws of thought, to predict performance in verbal learning experiments, and for many other purposes. There is a huge research literature on the use of word associations, but only a small part of this work is directly applicable to the problem of denotative meaning as considered here.

Most relevant to our present interests is the work of the psychologist James Deese on "the structure of associative meaning." This work is cogently summarized in an article by that title (1962) and in a later article (1964), and is extensively and lucidly discussed in a book by Deese, *The Structure of Associations in Language and Thought* (1965). To approach this work, let us consider the word association experiment in more detail.

A basic technique in word association experiments is to present a list of words to a large number of subjects, instructing each subject to respond to each stimulus word with a single response word. One then has a list of the responses given to each stimulus word together with the frequency with which each response occurred. For example, in the classic Kent and Rosanoff study of 1910, one thousand subjects gave responses to the stimulus word *chair*, as shown in Table 1.

I think you can see from this single listing of responses to one word why word associations have intrigued psychologists for so long. In a few minutes of thought you can probably come up with many of the experimental questions which have occupied psychologists. For example: Why do some people give such unusual responses? How do responses to different words compare? How do different groups of subjects compare? How do children and adults differ? How quickly to people respond? How can associations be classified? You can find discussion of such issues in volumes by Cofer (1961), Cofer and Musgrave (1963), Osgood (1953), and on the pages of the *Journal of Verbal Learning and Verbal Behavior*.

For our purposes we will be concerned with only a few of the many possible research questions dealing with word associations. The most interesting one in the present context is the last one raised above: How can associations be classified? There have been many diverse attempts to classify associations. For example, George Miller presents the following list (1951, p. 179):

> *contrast*: wet-dry, black-white, man-woman
> *similar*: blossom-flower, pain-hurt, swift-fast
> *subordinate*: animal-dog, man-father
> *coordinate*: apple-peach, dog-cat, man-boy
> *superordinate*: spinach-vegetable, man-male
> *assonance*: pack-tack, bread-red
> *part-whole*: petal-flower, day-week
> *completion*: forward-march, black-board
> *egocentricism*: success-I must, lonesome-never
> *word derivatives*: run-running, deep-depth
> *predication*: dog-bark, room-dark

TABLE 1   FIRST RESPONSES TO STIMULUS WORD *CHAIR*[1]

Frequency of Response	Response	Frequency of Response	Response
191	table	2	broken, hickory, home, necessity, oak, rounds, seating, use
127	seat		
108	sit		
83	furniture		
56	sitting		
49	wood	1	back, beauty, bed, book, boy, bureau, caning, careful, carpet, cart, color, crooked, cushions, feet, foot, footstool, form, Governor Winthrop, hair, implement, joiner, lunch, massive, mission, myself, object, occupy, office, people, place, placed, plant, idleness, platform, pleasant, pleasure, posture, reading, rubber, size, spooning, stand, stoop, study, support, tables, talk, teacher, timber, tool, upholstered, upholstery, white
45	rest		
38	stool		
21	comfort		
17	rocker		
15	rocking		
13	bench		
12	cushion		
11	legs		
10	floor		
9	desk, room		
8	comfortable		
7	ease, leg		
6	easy, sofa, wooden		
5	couch, hard, Morris, seated, soft		
4	arm, article, brown, high		
3	cane, convenience, house, large, low, lounge, mahogany, person, resting, rug, settee, useful		

Reprinted from *The American Journal of Insanity*, volume 67, pp. 317–390, 1910, by permission of the American Psychiatric Association.
[1]Based on Kent, G. H., and Rosanoff, A. J. A study of association in insanity. *Amer. J. Insanity*, 1910, *67*, 317–390.

These classifications are ingenious, but one wonders where they can lead to, how they can be determined, and when they can end. Miller throws up his hands and concludes: "Apparently words are related to one another in an amazing number of ways." Clearly, an attempt is being made in these various classifications to reveal some semantic attributes or dimensions, but the attempt is rather dissatisfying. Deese has pointed out that such classifications are not really revealed by the data of word associations themselves:

The classification schemes are partly psychological, partly logical, partly linguistic, and partly philosophic (epistemological). These classifications are more often than not rooted outside the association process itself and applied to that process by brute force. They attempt to impose upon associations the relations found in grammars, dictionaries of various sorts, and psychodynamic theories, as well as views about the organization of the physical world (1965, p. 22).

Deese himself (along with psychologists such as Jenkins, Cofer, Bousfield, and others), has been interested in entire *networks* of associated words, rather than simply looking at the responses to a given word in isolation. That is, words which serve as stimuli and response for each other also elicit a number of other words in common, and these other words, in turn, may serve as stimuli to elicit the original pair of words as responses. The interest is thus in relations between words. This should become clearer as we consider some examples.

Deese advances the notion of "associative meaning"—that is, the meaning represented by the range of response words elicited by a given stimulus word. If two words have the identical distribution of associative responses, then they would be considered to have the same associative meaning. In fact, of course, words will have *overlapping* collections of associative responses, and thus similarity in the associative meanings of two words can be measured in terms of overlapping distributions of associates to these two words.

As an example of relatedness, or associative overlap between two words, consider the responses made to the stimulus words *moth* and *butterfly* by fifty subjects. For computational purposes, the assumption is made that a word always first elicits itself, as a "representational response," and then elicits other response words. Thus, in Table 2, the numbers below *moth* represent the frequency with which each word in the left-hand column was given as a response to *moth* (e.g., *moth* elicited *butterfly* once, *insect* once, and so on). Similarly, the frequencies of response words to *butterfly* are given under that word. Only responses which the two words had in common are listed. Frequency of associative overlap is given in the last column.

While the details of calculation may not be completely clear to you from this brief example, the important thing to note is that this measure allows one to compute the degree to which two words elicit the same responses. For example, the associative overlap between *moth* and *insect* is 12—quite close to the overlap of 15 between *moth* and *butterfly*; the associative overlap between *butterfly* and *insect* is also 12. On the other

TABLE 2 ASSOCIATIVE OVERLAP BETWEEN *MOTH* AND *BUTTERFLY*[1]

Response Words	Stimulus Word moth	butterfly	Associative Overlap
moth	50	7	7
butterfly	1	50	1
insect	1	6	1
wings	2	5	2
fly	10	4	4
			15

Reprinted from *The Structure of Associations in Language and Thought* by James Deese.
Copyright © 1965 by The Johns Hopkins Press and reprinted with their permission.
[1]Based on Deese (1965).

hand, the overlap between *moth* and *flower* is 0, while that between *butterfly* and *flower* is 6.

If one picks an entire matrix of words which one suspects of having interesting interrelations (the choice of words is very important here), one can carry out a complex intercorrelational procedure called factor analysis in order to discover different clusters of words which share associates. These clusters of words often seem to define basic semantic categories. For example, Deese intercorrelated the relative common frequencies of responses to the following 19 words: *moth, insect, wing, bird, fly, yellow, flower, bug, cocoon, color, blue, bees, summer, sunshine, garden, sky, nature, spring, butterfly.* Factor analysis revealed the following different clusters of significant intercorrelations:

(1) "words having to do with animate creation" (*moth, insect, wing, bird, fly, bug, cocoon, bees, butterfly*)

(2) "words that do not have to do with animate things" (*yellow, flower, color, blue, summer, sunshine, garden, sky, nature, spring*)

(3) a division of animate words into two groups:
    (a) *wing, birds, bees, fly*
    (b) *bug, cocoon, moth, butterfly*

(4) a division of inanimate words into two groups:
    (a) *summer, sunshine, garden, flower, spring*
    (b) *blue, sky, yellow, color*

Reprinted from *The Structure of Associations in Language and Thought* by James Deese, by permission of The John Hopkins Press.

It is indeed striking that these patterns of intercorrelations of word associations reveal such basic semantic markers as *animate-inanimate*, as well as the more subtle and suggestive subdivisions appearing in (3) and (4). Deese has done extensive work of this sort on the associative structures of numerous nouns and adjectives. He has found, for example, that a large number of common antonymic adjectives strongly tend to elicit each other as responses, thus providing a collection of basic semantic polarities, as shown in Table 3.

TABLE 3   WORDS THAT FORM CONTRASTING PAIRS BY ELICITING ONE ANOTHER AS PRIMARIES[1]

alone	—	together	hard	—	soft
active	—	passive	heavy	—	light
alive	—	dead	high	—	low
back	—	front	inside	—	outside
bad	—	good	large	—	small
big	—	little	left	—	right
black	—	white	long	—	short
bottom	—	top	married	—	single
clean	—	dirty	narrow	—	wide
cold	—	hot	new	—	old
dark	—	light	old	—	young
deep	—	shallow	poor	—	rich
dry	—	wet	pretty	—	ugly
easy	—	hard	right	—	wrong
empty	—	full	rough	—	smooth
far	—	near	short	—	tall
fast	—	slow	sour	—	sweet
few	—	many	strong	—	weak
first	—	last	thick	—	thin
happy	—	sad			

Reprinted from *The Structure of Associations in Language and Thought* by James Deese,
Copyright © 1965 by The Johns Hopkins Press and reprinted with their permission.
[1]From Deese (1965, p. 123).

In the last chapter of his book, Deese discusses the cognitive operations which seem to underlie the sort of data he has analyzed. Of particular interest here is his emphasis on grouping and opposition as basic meaningful relations. In his words:

> The data on associative distributions suggest that the two fundamental operations we have for sorting out meaningful—that is, logical and syntactical relations among words—are contrast and grouping. We can establish the position of any given element in a language within the larger vocabulary of the language by contrasting it with some element or elements and/or by grouping it with respect to some other element or elements (1965, p. 164).

The notion of polarity, as represented in Table 3, appears to be a linguistic universal. That is, all languages make use of antonyms. This fact has been used by the psycholinguist Charles Osgood in constructing the "semantic differential," a pencil-and-paper device which asks people to rate concepts along a number of antonym scales. This technique has been used in a range of different languages and cultures (Osgood, 1964), and has proven to be an interesting and subtle tool in comparing attitudes towards certain concepts in various cultures. Osgood has found that antonyms break into three major, universal categories of affective or connotative meaning: evaluative (represented by dimensions such as *good-bad, happy-sad, beautiful-ugly*), potency (e.g., *strong-weak, brave-cowardly, hard-soft*), and activity (e.g., *fast-slow, tense-relaxed, hot-cold*) (Osgood et al., 1957).

The notion of grouping has been revealed by associative techniques, as discussed above. Grouping of words in semantic fields has also been demonstrated in very interesting fashion by another psychological technique, to which we now turn.

Semantic Generalization.   The basic idea of the semantic generalization technique comes from the study of conditioned responses: because clusters of words have come to be associated on semantic grounds, responses established to part of the cluster can be elicited by other parts of the cluster. That is, a response conditioned to a word can generalize to other words on the basis of their semantic relations. This technique was developed in the Soviet Union in the twenties, and has had an important influence in the development of Soviet psycholinguistic theory (see Slobin, 1966*b*).

A variety of both voluntary and involuntary responses has been used in the Soviet research. As an example of semantic generalization of a conditioned involuntary response, let us first consider experiments carried out by Shvartz (1964) using a photochemical response—reduction in the sensitivity of peripheral vision in response to a flash of light. With a word as conditioned stimulus, response will generalize to words of closely related meaning. But words of similar sound only at first produce the conditioned response, and then become differentiated and cease to do so. Thus a response conditioned to the Russian word *doktor* ('doctor') will be evoked by a word like *vrach* ('physician'), but not by a word of similar sound but unrelated meaning, like *diktor* ('announcer').[1] Shvartz

[1]As Soviet psychologists have frequently pointed out, this sort of conditioned behavior is strikingly different from that observed in experiments with animals. If an animal is conditioned to give a response to a certain tone, for example, he will generalize his response to sounds related to the original tone on some physical continuum (like pitch). Generalization in adult human beings, in experiments such as the above, is not along physical, but semantic continua. It is interesting to note that very young children respond to words of similar sound rather than those of similar meaning in such experiments, as do adults when they are fatigued, ill, or under the influence of drugs which suppress activity of higher cortical centers. Feeble-minded individuals also show response generalization on the basis of the sounds of words, rather than their meanings. Thus the phenomenon of semantic generalization reflects a relatively mature and highly developed level of cortical functioning. (See Slobin, 1966*b*.)

considers synonyms, such as *doctor* and *physician*, as identical stimuli, since each of them, though with different sounds, calls into play the same cortical connections established in previous experience in medical contexts.

The work of Luria and Vinogradova (1959) is especially interesting in that it seems to reveal *levels* of relatedness of meanings in semantic fields. Subjects were given electric shock upon the presentation of a given word in a series, and the generalization of vasomotor responses to other words was tested. It was found that subjects made an involuntary *defense* response (vasoconstriction of the blood vessels of both the finger and the forehead) to words close in meaning to the word on which they received shock, and that they made an involuntary *orienting* response (vasoconstriction in the finger and vasodilation in the forehead) to words more distantly related to the critical word. For example, if a subject was given a shock to the word *violin*, he made a similar defense reaction to such words as *violinist*, *bow*, *string*, *mandolin*, and others. He made an orienting response to names of stringless musical instruments, such as *accordion* and *drum*, and to other words connected with music, such as *sonata* and *concert*. In addition, of course, there were neutral words to which the subject made no autonomic response.

This experiment revealed not only the existence of complex semantic structures, but also the fact that the subjects themselves were largely unconscious of such structures in the experiment. While they responded consistently on an involuntary response basis, when interviewed after the experiment they were usually not aware of obvious semantic clusters of words to which they had responded.

These few examples show that semantic generalization is an intriguing method for the study of meaning. As yet it has not been extensively used in this country (but see Feather, 1965), and data from this technique have only rarely been compared with analyses of word meaning and word relatedness based on other techniques. Much research remains to be done here.

Sentence Meaning

Where does all of this work on components and dimensions of word meaning fit into the grammatical model which we have been considering in this book? In Chapter 1 we observed that knowledge of syntactic structure was necessary for the comprehension of sentences. But, clearly, you must also know what the words of a sentence mean in order to interpret it. Furthermore, the meaning of a word can depend on its syntactic context. Consider, for example, how the context of an entire sentence can subtly shift the meaning of a single word:

(1) I would have taken the plane but it was too heavy to carry.

It is the task of the semantic component of the grammar to assign interpretations to sentences. In order to carry out this task, it is evident that the semantic component must take account of *both* syntactic structures of sentences and semantic structures of words. How this is done is not at all clear in present-day linguistics. In 1957 Chomsky was able to write: "Grammar is best formulated as a self-contained study independent of semantics" (p. 106). By 1965 it was necessary for him to point out: "In fact, it should not be taken for granted, necessarily, that syntactic and semantic considerations can be sharply distinguished" (p. 77). A number of Chomsky's followers have carried the argument for semantics even further in recent years. For example, McCawley stated in 1968: ". . . a full account of English syntax requires a fairly full account of semantics to just as great an extent as the converse is true" (p. 161).

In short, the line between syntax and semantics has become very hazy indeed. For example, consider the sentence:

(2) Abstractness respects Chomsky.

This sentence is deviant because *respects* is the sort of verb which must take a human subject, and *abstractness* is nonhuman. But is the feature "human" to be considered a syntactic feature, limiting the subject nouns of *respect*? If this is the case, then the sentence is not grammatical. Or is the feature "human" better considered a semantic feature, in which case the sentence *is* grammatical, in the strictly syntactic sense, though anomalous. It seems that as syntactic analysis becomes more and more detailed and precise, the features which restrict combinations of words in sentences look more and more semantic. In fact, they begin to look like the basic semantic components we have just been considering. One encounters features such as "animate," "human," "evaluative," "reversible process," and linguists will disagree as to whether such features are syntactic or semantic, both or neither.

We are not in a position to resolve such abstruse and delicate problems here. But it is of interest to note the re-occurrence, in this discussion, of basic semantic features. These features must also play a role in the interpretation of deviant sentences—an ability of great psycholinguistic interest, which is as yet little understood. The deviant sentence presented above, "Abstractness respects Chomsky," probably did not simply leave your mind in a meaningless blur. In fact, this sentence is rather easy to interpret if you attribute to *abstractness* the features required by the verb *respect*. Thus *abstractness* becomes something animate—perhaps the "spirit of abstraction"—who can then, indeed, "respect Chomsky."

This ability to interpret deviant sentences is yet another aspect of psycholinguistic competence which must someday be accounted for in detail. Katz and Fodor (1963), in developing an early version of semantic theory within transformational grammar, pointed out additional aspects of linguistic competence which must be accounted for. These aspects go beyond the sort of syntactic competence outlined in Chapter 1, but you will note certain formal similarities between the accounts of syntactic and semantic competence. Just as we are able to recognize syntactic ambiguity (e.g., "Visiting relatives can be a nuisance"), we must be able to recognize *semantic ambiguity* in sentences which are not ambiguous in their syntax. The first half of sentence (1), for example, contains a semantic ambiguity in regard to multiple meanings of the word *take*. Katz and Fodor offer a similar example:

(3) The bill is large.

This sentence has but one underlying syntactic analysis, yet it clearly has more than one meaning, because of the multiple meanings of the word *bill*. The ambiguity is removed when the sentence is extended to:

(4) The bill is large but need not be paid.

Thus you are able to "disambiguate" parts of a sentence in terms of other parts, and in this way determine the number of possible meanings of a sentence. You are able to make use of semantic relations in the sentence to eliminate potential ambiguities.

Sentence (2) demonstrated another aspect of semantic competence —namely, the ability to recognize (and sometimes to interpret) anomaly. Yet another semantic ability which Katz and Fodor have pointed out is the ability to make paraphrases—to relate the meanings of sentences which have very different structures.

Although we cannot present a well-developed model of semantic competence here, it should be possible at least to guess about what some of its major components might be. First of all, a semantic theory must have a dictionary (or lexicon). A dictionary is needed, obviously, because some words have more or less the same meaning, and some have distinctly different meanings. The syntactic component of the grammar cannot account for the fact that some sentences which differ by a single word are interpreted as different in meaning (e.g., "The tiger bit me" and "The mouse bit me"), while other sentences, which also differ only by one word, are interpreted as (more or less) identical in meaning (e.g., "The oculist examined me" and "The eye doctor examined me").[2]

---

[2]Note that here we come up against the controversial question of just what is meant by "same in meaning." These two sentences may be the same referentially, but they may have different meanings on other levels. For example, you can tell something about what sort of person someone is on the basis of whether he says *oculist* or *eye doctor*. This is another sort of meaning which words and sentences have: people learn to use certain stylistic variants in certain situations, and the style of a man's language tells you much about his personality and social position. All of this, of course, is far beyond the more limited task posed above of distinguishing unambiguous sentences from ambiguous and anomalous sentences. Eventually, a full model of the language-user will have to include sociolinguistic rules as well as linguistic and psycholinguistic rules. For example, consider the following range of sentences. They all have the same social meaning in that they are all requests to convey a salt shaker along a table. But there is no linguistic theory which could class them together on the basis of their referential meaning, and there is no well-developed sociolinguistic theory which could adequately describe the range of social meanings expressed: "Gimme the salt!" "Please pass the salt." "I wonder if you'd be good enough to pass the salt." "Would there be any salt at your end of the table?"

The dictionary must characterize the meanings of words in some way, perhaps according to basic semantic components, as discussed above. Furthermore, it will probably have to differentiate meanings on the basis of the different syntactic roles which a given word can perform. Take, for example, the word *play*. It can be used as a noun or as a verb or as an adjective. In interpreting a sentence in which the word *play* appears, first of all the syntactic analysis will provide information in regard to the syntactic function of *play* in the given sentence (e.g., a noun in "That was a good play"). In further interpreting "That was a good play" one would then have to deal only with the noun senses of the word *play*. According to this approach (cf. Katz and Fodor, 1963; Katz and Postal, 1964), the dictionary entry for a word would have first a grammatical marker, and then, for each grammatical marker, there would be a list of senses of the word. For example, *play* as a noun could mean a theatrical performance, a sequence of moves in some athletic sport, and so on. The basic components of meaning — whatever they may be — would have to play some role in characterizing word senses.

Another component which would be required in a semantic theory would be a set of rules (Katz and Fodor call them "projection rules") which take account of relations between words in the sentence in order to determine which senses of each word could be appropriate in the context of a given sentence — that is, which combinations of word meanings would result in a meaningful, nonanomalous sentence. (If there were no possible combination, of course, the sentence would be anomalous. And if there were more than one nonanomalous combination of word meaning, then the sentence would be ambiguous.)

A full model of psycholinguistic competence could not limit itself to the context of the individual sentence. Two other sorts of context must be involved in sentence understanding: the context of discourse (other sentences) and the nonlinguistic context of objects, people, and events. Many sentences which may be ambiguous or incomplete in themselves, take on meaning in the larger context of communication. By now, however, we have gone far beyond the grasp of current theories of language. The use of language in social contexts is beginning to be systematically explored by philosophers of language (cf. Searle, 1969) and sociolinguists (cf. Gumperz and Hymes, in press). Here we have another frontier which promises to be developed in the seventies.

Up until this point we have reviewed work on the structure and organization of meaning without involving ourselves in theories of the behavioral processes underlying the meaningful use of language. Psychologists, however, have had a long-standing concern with the characterization of such processes. A critical examination of the historical development of treatments of this problem by American psychologists will cast light on important underlying trends in behaviorism.

PROCESS APPROACHES TO MEANING

American behavioral psychologists, in studying what they have called "meaning," have almost entirely limited themselves to the problem of reference, which is a limited aspect of the general problem of linguistic meaning. That is, they have been mainly concerned with associations between words and the objects and events to which they refer. For many psychologists (e.g., Osgood, 1953 and his followers) the task has been defined as determining mediating processes within people which link words and things. Fodor (1965) has pointed out, however, that while all behaviorist theories have derived meaning from thing naming: (1) not all words name things; (2) the nature of "things" is often not immediately given in experience; (3) thing-naming words usually have varied referents; and (4) meaning varies with speech context. We will return to these points later. For now, let us limit ourselves to the problem of reference and see how far we can get.

One classical way of looking at the problem of reference is to use Ogden and Richards' "triangle of reference," which comes from their famous book of the twenties, *The Meaning of Meaning* (1923):

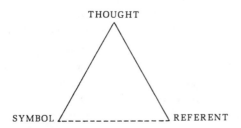

According to Ogden and Richards there are three components in every referential process: a *symbol,* a *thought,* and a *referent.* There is a connection between symbol and thought, and between thought and referent. But the connection between symbol and referent must always be indirect: it is a connection which exists in the human mind.

"Thought" in this diagram is some sort of psychological process which goes on when a person relates a symbol and a referent. (Ogden and Richards call this process "interpretation"). The connection between symbols and referents (or words and things) is arbitrary. That is, there is no *necessary* connection between symbols and the nonlinguistic world. That is why the base of the triangle is a dotted line. (There is apparently a natural and universal feeling that this should not be the case. Word magic and nominal realism are widespread phenomena, deplored by philosophers, and found in all ages and places — including our own.) Our concern here, however, is with another part of that triangle. I think you can look at the history of psychological approaches to the processes underlying meaning in terms of what to put at the *apex* of the triangle: what to put inside the "black box" as a middle term between symbols and referents. The history of philosophy and psychology is filled with a variety of alternatives for what Ogden and Richards have labelled "thought" in their diagram:

"image" (Locke, Titchener)

"disposition" (Charles Morris)

"response" (John B. Watson)

"fractional response" (Charles Osgood)

American psychologists have generally tried to set up some kind of action or response as the third term between symbol and referent. The only exception which readily comes to mind is Titchener and his imagistic theory of thought and meaning—but Titchener was always somewhat of an anomaly in American psychology. He was the one major American psychologist who tried to keep European continental psychology going on this continent in the early part of this century—and without much success in terms of a following after his death. Otherwise, there is a long tradition in American theories of man to look at action as the essence of being. There are many interesting sociocultural explanations of why this should be the case (e.g., the frontier, the Protestant Ethic, emergent capitalism and industrialism)—but, at any rate, this basic attitude can be traced back at least to American philosophy at the end of the last century. In regard to the referential process, this attitude has been characterized by attempts to look at reference in terms of what a symbol causes a person to do. The approach has its roots in the pragmatism of Peirce and James and Dewey. Peirce, for example, suggested that the sentence, "This is hard" means something like, "If you try to scratch this, you will fail." The underlying notion was that meaning is tied to the performance of certain operations; that symbols have consequences in human action.

This pragmatic philosophy is congenial to psychologists who wish to emphasize the *active, operational, behavioral* aspects of meaning, as opposed to its *passive, introspective, subjective* aspects. Since the First World War, behavioristic theories of meaning have developed in America in consonance with these notions of pragmatism, and in consonance with Pavlovian conditioning theory. John B. Watson's behaviorism, which he proposed in 1913, developed in close connection with the work of Pavlov and his school.[3] The behavioristic theories of meaning

---

[3]It is of interest to note, in passing, that Soviet psychology is based on similar pragmatic premises—and probably due to very similar sociocultural determinants in the recent histories of the USA and the USSR. One of the guiding principles of Soviet psychology today is that man perceives the world only by acting purposively upon it. Soviet psychologists believe, along with Watson and Osgood, that meaning is ultimately based on active responding to things and events.

have looked for a response to mediate between symbol and referent. Response theories of meaning, however, have had a peculiar history. At first, Watson proposed a "substitution theory." To him, words had meanings because they were responded to in the same way as one would respond to their referents. The responses involved were gross, observable, and peripheral in the early psychological studies — responses like movements of the hands, mouth, throat, and other parts of the body. Osgood (1952) reviews this work of the twenties and thirties, summarizing its ambiguity and general failure. It became clear that people do not respond to a word in the same way as they respond to its referent. That is, when you hear the word apple you do not begin to make apple-eating responses as you would in response to a real apple.

Accordingly, the responses which are considered to be the meanings of words have become smaller and smaller and have retreated into the brain. That is, perhaps you only make minimal apple-eating responses when you hear the word *apple*; or perhaps you only think of making those responses. And so the response theory of meaning progressed from a theory of *overt* responses to a theory of *implicit* muscular responses, then to *fractional* responses, and finally, in Osgood's mediation theory, the meaning of a word can be a tiny segment of a response which occurs totally within the central nervous system.[4]

This is a puzzling evolution. It began, in Anglo-American psychology, with John Locke, who spoke of images in the mind. Behaviorists eventually arose to object to such unobservable mental variables, and pulled these images out to the peripheral musculature, calling them responses. Now, in current neo-behaviorism, they are still called "responses," but no longer can be measured in any objective way, since they can take place unobserved in the "black box" of the head. They are not even available to introspection, as images were.

What has happened, then, to the response theory of meaning? Is a "fractional mediating response" any more objective or scientific a concept than "image" or "thought" or "disposition"? Does calling it a "response" make anything about the problem of meaning more clear to us? I think that, by and large, you can understand most of the current theo-

---

[4]The term "mediational" is used because the internal, intervening response can, in itself, become a stimulus for action. For example, the word *fire* was originally associated with actual fires. By conditioning, the word itself can later come to elicit part of the response originally made to fire (e.g., fear). This is called a "mediating response" (r_m). Such a response is considered "representational" because it is part of the behavior produced by the original stimulus (i.e., the real fire). According to the theory, representational responses produce "self-stimulation" (s_m) which can then become the stimulus for new, overt responses. Thus, in the future, the word *fire* can call forth escape responses through the mediation of the fear responses associated with that word in past experience. Osgood attempts to account for meaning in terms of such $r_m - s_m$ processes. (For a refutation of this position see Fodor, 1965.)

rizing about meaning in experimental psychology by substituting the word "image" for "response." And this throws you right back into the ancient philosophical problems of the nature of images in thought. (For a discussion in relation to reference and meaning, see Brown, 1958, Chapter 3.)

Behaviorists themselves have come to lose the distinction between overt, measurable response and inner state, as you can read in the following quotes from the behavioristic accounts of meaning offered by Staats, Skinner, and Mowrer:

> . . . word meaning may be classically conditioned in the same manner as other responses, and thus word meaning may be considered a response. . . . Many stimulus objects may be considered UCSs [unconditioned stimuli] in terms of the sensory responses they elicit. For example, a visual stimulus may be considered to elicit a "seeing" response in the individual in the sense that seeing the object is a response. An auditory stimulus may be considered to elicit a "hearing" response, a tactual stimulus to elicit a "feeling" response, and so on.
>
> Several studies . . . indicate that portions of such sensory responses may be conditioned. Skinner (1953) has discussed how sensory responses can come to be elicited by formerly neutral stimuli on the basis of classical conditioning.
>
> A man may see or hear "stimuli which are not present" on the pattern of the conditioned reflex; he may see X, not only when X is present, but when any stimulus which has frequently accompanied X is present. The dinner bell not only makes our mouth water, it makes us see food.
>
> (Staats and Staats, 1963, p. 266.)
>
> . . . [W]e may confidently assume that the light . . . produces a light *sensation* . . . which is conditionable in the form of a light *image.* Such a reaction, to be sure, is central, or "cognitive," rather than overt, behavioral . . . (Mowrer, 1960, p. 282).

We are thus clearly thrown all the way back to an image theory of meaning. As Brown points out (1958) such theories are plagued by several persistent problems: (1) words refer to categories, not to particular things, and what would a picture of a category look like? (2) Many people report that they do not have mental images for all the words they know and use. (3) And even when people do report mental images as meanings for words, the images do not contain all the information required to specify the meaning of the word. The psychologist Titchener, for example, had the following image for the word *meaning*: "the blue-gray tip of a kind of scoop which has a bit of yellow about it (probably a part of the handle) and which is just digging into a dark mass of what appears to be plastic material" (Brown, 1958, p. 90).

A cognitive psychologist can express some pleasure in discovering that even behaviorists are forced to introduce cognitive terms into their accounts (even if these terms do tend to occur between quotation marks!), but images do not seem to be the most useful cognitive constructs to account for the psychological processes involved in understanding the meanings of words. By the time a behaviorist is forced to talk about "seeing responses," the terminology of experimental psychology seems to have been stretched beyond reasonable limits.

Is there any gain at all, then, to maintaining the terminology of response psychology in discussing the psychological processes underlying meaning? Staats, Osgood, and others have made the claim that this approach is useful because it allows for the application of established laws of conditioning to the study of meaning. However, the evidence of the applicability of such laws to the study of meaning is quite slim. One of the major appeals in supporting this position deals with the puzzling phenomenon of "semantic satiation" (cf. Osgood, 1963). If you say a word over and over again, it loses its meaning for a while. Osgood argues that if meaning is a response to a verbal stimulus, it can indeed extinguish upon repeated presentations of the stimulus. Following Hullian learning theory, "reactive inhibition" accumulates upon repeated pairings of stimulus and response, bringing about temporary inhibition of response. If you consider the meaning of a word to be some sort of response to the sound or uttering of a word, then, following Hullian theory, the meaning of the word (i.e., the response) should be temporarily inhibited upon repeated arousal.

If this is a major piece of evidence that meaning is a response, it is a slender reed indeed upon which to base an entire theory.[5] The response

---

[5]The only other evidence Osgood offers for the response theory of the meaning is the phenomenon of semantic generalization. The argument is that if a number of different stimuli (i.e., words) evoke a common response (i.e., meaning), they are equivalent stimuli, and a response conditioned to one such word will generalize to other words by means of internal mediating responses of the sort described by Osgood. For example, in the Shvartz experiment discussed above, the response conditioned to the word *doctor* is actually conditioned to the self-stimulation (s_m) aroused by the meaning response (r_m). The word *physician* arouses the same internal mediating events ($r_m - s_m$) as does the word *doctor*, and hence also evokes the response conditioned to *doctor*. Again, it is evident that the theory falls in the presence of alternative plausible explanations of semantic generalization, which are not hard to come by. In addition, the argument from semantic generalization studies totally fails to account for the fact that different words *do* have different meanings. In the Luria and Vinogradova experiment, for example, a response conditioned to the word *violin* generalized to such words as *bow*, *string*, *violinist*, and *mandolin*. Following Osgood's argument, one would have to claim that these words are all synonyms.

theory of meaning could be seriously called into question, then, if we had even one alternative plausible explanation of the phenomenon of semantic satiation. Harriet Amster (1964) has clearly pointed up many of the methodological problems in interpreting semantic satiation experiments, and shows that alternative explanations are possible. She opts for an "adaptation level" explanation:

> This formulation provides that judgments are made with respect to internal norms, adaptation levels, which can be objectively and quantitatively specified. . . . When a stimulus in the absence of any context other than itself is repeated continuously, the adaptation level shifts gradually during repetition or exposure until it is equal to the value of the stimulus . . . a stimulus should be judged as neutral on all dimensions of connotation [i.e., meaningless in Osgood's sense] as frequency of exposure in a uniform context is increased (p. 283).

The phenomenon of semantic satiation illustrates a deeper point, which we have touched on before. Amster hints at this point when she speaks of "a stimulus in the absence of any context other than itself." The point is simply that a word in isolation has no one particular meaning. A meaning exists in a context: it is assigned to a word by a context. We will return to this matter of word meaning in context again. But note first that even if we accept the naïve notions that meaning can be limited to reference, and that the referential process is an internal event aroused by a given word, we have not succeeded in finding a satisfactory model. Thus in regard to American psychology's main claim to have explained the nature of meaning (actually the nature of reference) we must chalk up a failure. No essential progress seems to have been made in this paradigm from eighteenth century British philosophy to twentieth century American psychology.

As pointed out earlier, however, this very paradigm of limiting meaning to the reference of individual, isolated words cannot be an adequate approach to meaning. Meaning could not simply be a response to things because (1) not all words name things; and, further, even if we were to deal only with thing-naming words, (2) most words have many meanings (thing-naming words usually have varied referents), and the particular meaning of a word varies with linguistic and nonlinguistic context; and, even in regard to words which do name things, (3) the nature of "things" is often not immediately given in experience, and must itself be learned. (That is, language itself may shape the way in which the child comes to categorize the world.)

The second point has two aspects, as discussed earlier in the chapter: words have multiple meanings, and the particular meaning is selected by the context of the utterance in which the word appears. The problem in terms of unique word meanings (e.g., a unique image, or response, or what have you, associated with a given word) is especially complicated in that the multiple meanings of a word may not even share any given common denominator. At first you may not agree with this proposition, but consider the following compelling examples offered by the linguist Nida (1958, p. 282):

> . . . we specifically reject meaning as 'a common denominator' or 'what is common to all situations in which a term is employed.' If, for example, we analyze the use of *charge* in the following contexts, we will find that a common denominator would be precious little indeed. It would be only a small part of the total meaning signalled by *charge* in the various contexts: charge into the line of players, charge the gun, charge the battery, charge the pencil, charge the man ten dollars, charge the culprit with the crime, he gets a charge out of it, a charge of electricity, he is in charge, he is a public charge. The only way to 'define' the meaning of *charge* is to describe (usually by illustrative phrases or sentences) the distribution of the word.

(Now try to build a psychological model in which the meaning of *charge* is a given mental image, or an internal mediating response; or in which a response conditioned to the utterance of *charge* generalizes to other words; or in which the repeated pronunciation of *charge* makes it sound meaningless for a while; and so forth.)

The role of multiple meanings gains additional significance in light of a striking fact: the more frequently a word is used, the more meanings it seems to have. Look in any dictionary and you will see many more listings under common than under uncommon words. For example, in one dictionary the word-form *case* has 23 meanings or senses; 69 meanings are listed for *take*; the word-form *free* has 38 meanings, and so on. Apparently people find it easier to learn and store a smaller number of words, each with many senses, than to learn and store a separate phonetic form for each sense. Given the large number of senses packed into common words, it must be that in understanding sentences we have some way of attending to specific meanings of potentially ambiguous words on the basis of how they are used. This is the point of the uses of context which has been made repeatedly throughout the chapter. The word *pen*, for example, has two clearly different meanings in the contexts of the sentences "The pig is in the pen" and "The ink is in the pen." The two interpretations must be based on the meanings of the other words in the sentences, because there are no syntactic or positional cues. In fact, the syntactic structure of the two sentences is identical. Sentence understanding thus clearly must have a semantic component, and this component must be realized in terms of some sort of psychological processes — as yet chiefly unknown.

The semantic component, of course, requires a syntactic component, which, as discussed earlier in the book, must also have some psychological realization. Consideration of the syntactic component may illuminate part of the problem of words which do not have concrete referents — at least those which perform grammatical functions. Take a word like *the*, for example, which does not seem to fit into the conceptual scheme of the triangle of reference at all. What is the referent of *the*? There isn't any, of course. For that matter, what thought, or what response, does *the* arouse in you? In me it arouses almost nothing at all, except perhaps a visual image of the written word itself (which is an accident of the fact that I happen to be literate, and not at all relevant to the basic psychological processes underlying meaning). Does this mean that the word *the* is meaningless? Of course not. All it means is that there are other kinds of meanings we need to study (perhaps we should call them "syntactic meanings").[6] A theory of the referential process — to repeat the theme — is not a complete theory of meaning. Such a theory is, unfortunately, neither available nor yet clearly discernible on the psycholinguistic horizon.

In the next chapter we will go beyond the limited questions examined here of word and sentence meaning to consider the role of language in cognitive growth and in the processes of adult cognition. As a final footnote, however, to the amazingly rich tangle of problems raised by the investigation of meaning, it may be best to return to the adventures of Alice:

> "When *I* use a word," Humpty Dumpty said, in rather a scornful tone, "it means just what I choose it to mean — neither more nor less."
>
> "The question is," said Alice, "whether you *can* make words mean so many different things."
>
> "The question is," said Humpty Dumpty, "which is to be master — that's all."
>
> Alice was too much puzzled to say anything. . . .

---

[6] The word *the* takes on meaning solely in the way it is used with other words. Its meaning is defined by its function. One of its functions, for example, is to signal that a noun is coming soon. Consider the following example, suggested by Bruner (unpublished lecture), of a telegraphic sentence, "Ship sails." Presented out of context in this way we don't know whether *ship* is a noun and *sails* a verb (a declarative sentence), or vice versa (an imperative sentence). If we insert *the* into the sentence to make it clear which word is the noun, though, the ambiguity disappears: "The ship sails" or "Ship the sails." It is evident, thus, that *the* is not meaningless.

5

Language and Cognition

The consistency of human behavior, such as it is, is due entirely to the fact that men have formulated their desires, and subsequently rationalized them, in terms of words. The verbal formulation of a desire will cause a man to go on pressing forward towards his goal, even when the desire itself lies dormant. Similarly, the rationalization of his desire in terms of some theological or philosophical system will convince him that he does well to persevere in this way. . . . From the psychological point of view, a theology or a philosophy may be defined as a device for permitting men to perform in cold blood and continuously actions which, otherwise, they could accomplish only by fits and starts and when the impulse was strong and hot within them. . . .

For evil, then, as well as for good, words make us the human beings we actually are. Deprived of language we should be as dogs or monkeys. Possessing language, we are men and women able to persevere in crime no less than in heroic virtue, capable of intellectual achievements beyond the scope of any animal, but at the same time capable of systematic silliness and stupidity such as no dumb beast could ever dream of.

—Aldous Huxley, "Words and their Meanings"
(in Black, 1962, pp. 4–5)

Human culture, social behavior, and thinking could not exist as we know them in the absence of language—as Aldous Huxley has so eloquently expressed above. In this chapter we shall attempt to refine these notions and follow up some of them in greater detail. More particularly, we want to know to what extent language may actively shape human thought and action. In regard to the growing child, we must determine the ways in which his ability to speak may affect the course of his mental development. And finally we will deal with an old and puzzling question: Do people who speak different languages think in different ways?

LANGUAGE, SPEECH, AND THOUGHT

To begin with: Are *thought* and *speech* inseparable? This ancient question still has not received a definitive answer in the annals of philosophy or psychology. The most extreme affirmative answer to the question was formulated by John B. Watson, the father of American behaviorist psychology: " . . . according to my view, thought processes are really motor habits in the larynx" (1913). American behaviorism, in its early days, was reluctant to postulate any intervening variables between stimulus and response; Watson's assertion that thought is no more than covert speaking is a clear reflection of this tendency.

A less extreme position has a rich history in Russian psychology. One of the earliest scientific positions taken on this problem was voiced in 1863 by Ivan M. Sechenov, the father of Russian physiology and mentor of Pavlov:

> When a child thinks he invariably talks at the same time. Thought in five-year-olds is mediated through words or whispers, surely through movements of the tongue and lips, which is also very frequently (perhaps always, but in different degrees) true of the thinking of adults (1863, p. 498).

The Russian position, then, is that language and thought are closely linked in childhood, but that, in the course of development, adult thinking becomes free of language in some ways—at least free of overt or covert *speech responses*. This position has been most significantly elaborated by the great Soviet psychologist of the 1930's. L. S. Vygotsky.

In his major work, *Thought and Language* (1962), first published in the USSR after his untimely death in 1934, Vygotsky developed the notion that in both phylogeny and ontogeny there are strains of nonverbal thought (e.g., "tool thought" involved in the solution of instrumental problems) and nonintellectual speech (e.g., emotional cries), and he attempted to trace the interacting development of these two strains until the point in man at which speech can serve thought and thought can be revealed in speech. We will return to Soviet research on these questions later in the chapter.

The brilliant work on cognitive development carried out by Jean Piaget and his colleagues in Geneva, Switzerland, presents a clear opposition to the behaviorist tradition. Piaget's school takes the position that cognitive development proceeds on its own, generally being followed by linguistic development, or finding reflection in the child's language. The child's intellect grows through interaction with the things and the people in his environment. To the extent that language is involved in these interactions, it may amplify or facilitate development in some cases, but it does not in itself bring about cognitive growth.

Before dealing with these questions of human development, however, we must determine whether any sort of intelligent, higher-order cognitive processes can occur in the absence of language. Some examples are in order.

First, we must be careful to remember the distinction between *language* and *speech* made at the beginning of the book. Speech is a tangible, physical process resulting in the production of speech sounds, while language is an intangible system of meanings and linguistic structures. Thus Watson's position does not deal with *language* and thought at all; rather, he equates *speech* and thought. Cognitive psychologists, like Vygotsky and Piaget, are concerned with speech and thought to the extent that speech is involved in communication of knowledge between people. But, more essentially, they are concerned with *language* and thought, that is, with the relations of inner linguistic and cognitive structures. To them, this inner use of language need not always be reflected in the articulatory movements of the vocal apparatus.

Many arguments have been raised against the strong Watsonian hypothesis (see, for example, Osgood, 1951). The most obvious criticism seems to come from the implication that a man deprived of contact with his speech musculature would lose the ability to think. Striking counterevidence to this reductio ad absurbum is presented by Cofer (1960, pp. 94–95):

> Smith *et al.* (1947) were interested in the question of what central depressing or analgesic properties are possessed by the drug Curare. Smith volunteered to be a subject of a study of this problem.

A form of Curare (*d*-tubocurarine) was administered to Smith in-
travenously. . . . Skeletal muscle paralysis was complete, and
oxygen and artificial respiration were required. The subject, of
course, after a time, was able to make no gestural or vocal responses. His report, dictated after recovery, was that he was "clear
as a bell" and knew what was going on; his recall for the things
said or done to him during the period of total paralysis was reported to be excellent. He was apparently able to solve simple
problems so long as there was any means of communication with
him, for example, by a thumb gesture after speech was gone. The
EEG was normal throughout and responded appropriately to pattern vision.

So much, then, for the naive equation of speech and thought. But is it
possible to *think* without *inner speech*—that is, without some internal
mediation of language, even if not overtly or covertly articulated? There
are a number of mental processes which seem to be prelinguistic or nonlinguistic. You are certainly familiar with the unpleasant phenomenon
of groping for a word, or trying to find the best way to express yourself.
No one has described this better than the great psychologist William
James in his famous textbook, *Psychology: Briefer Course* (1892, pp.
163–164):

Suppose we try to recall a forgotten name. The state of our consciousness is peculiar. There is a gap therein; but no mere gap. It
is a gap that is intensely active. A sort of wraith of the name is in
it, beckoning us in a given direction, making us at moments tingle
with the sense of our closeness, and then letting us sink back
without the longed-for term. If wrong names are proposed to us,
this singularly definite gap acts immediately so as to negate them.
They do not fit into its mould. And the gap of one word does not
feel like the gap of another, all empty of content as both might
seem necessarily to be when described as gaps. When I vainly try
to recall the name of Spalding, my consciousness is far removed
from what it is when I vainly try to recall the name of Bowles.
There are innumerable consciousnesses of *want*, no one of which
taken in itself has a name, but all different from each other. . . .
The rhythm of a lost word may be there without a sound to clothe
it; or the evanescent sense of something which is the initial vowel
or consonant may mock us fitfully, without growing more distinct.
Every one must know the tantalizing effect of the blank rhythm of
some forgotten verse, restlessly dancing in one's mind, and striv-
ing to be filled out with words.

. . . And has the reader never asked himself what kind of a
mental fact is his *intention of saying a thing* before he has said it?

It is an entirely definite intention, distinct from all other intentions, an absolutely distinct state of consciousness, therefore; and yet how much of it consists of definite sensorial images, either of words or of things? Hardly anything! Linger, and the words and things come into the mind; the anticipatory intention, the divination is there no more. But as the words that replace it arrive, it welcomes them successively and calls them right if they agree with it, it rejects them and calls them wrong if they do not. The intention *to-say-so-and-so* is the only name it can receive. One may admit that a good third of our psychic life consists in these rapid premonitory perspective views of schemes of thought not yet articulate.

In what form are these intentions and feelings? Certainly they are thoughts, and certainly they are not yet linguistic. Why would we ever have to grope for words if thought were no more than simply a matter of inner speech? This problem was clearly discussed by Vygotsky (1962):

The flow of thought is not accompanied by a simultaneous unfolding of speech. The two processes are not identical, and there is no rigid correspondence between the units of thought and speech. This is especially obvious when a thought process miscarries — when, as Dostoevski puts it, a thought "will not enter words." Thought has its own structure, and the transition from it to speech is no easy matter.

Vygotsky expressed the matter well when he said: "Thought is not merely expressed in words; it comes into existence through them." For Vygotsky, inner speech is not just subvocal uttering of sentences, as it was for Watson; it is a special form of speech, lying between thought and vocal speech, as he discusses so clearly in his classic book, *Thought and Language* (1962):

Thought, unlike speech, does not consist of separate units. When I wish to communicate the thought that today I saw a barefoot boy in a blue shirt running down the street, I do not see every item separately . . . I conceive of all this in one thought, but I put it into separate words. A speaker often takes several minutes to disclose one thought. In his mind the whole thought is present at once, but in speech it has to be developed successively. A thought may be compared to a cloud shedding a shower of words.

Another very intriguing line of evidence about the independence of much of thought from verbal formulation comes from the statements of great scientists, mathematicians, and artists about their creative thought.

A little book by Brewster Ghiselin, *The Creative Process* (1955), is full of rich examples of an initial period of "incubation" of an idea or problem, followed by a sudden resolution, after which the creator is faced with the tremendous difficulty of putting the result of his thinking into the verbal medium. The introspections of Albert Einstein in this regard are especially illuminating (in Ghiselin, 1955, p. 43):

> The words of the language, as they are written or spoken, do not seem to play any role in my mechanism of thought. The psychical entities which seem to serve as elements in thought are certain signs and more or less clear images which can be "voluntarily" reproduced and combined.
>
> There is, of course, a certain connection between those elements and relevant logical concepts. It is also clear that the desire to arrive at logically connected concepts is the emotional basis of this rather vague play with the above mentioned elements. But taken from a psychological viewpoint, this combinatory play seems to be the essential feature in productive thought—before there is any connection with logical construction in words or other kinds of signs which can be communicated to others.
>
> The above mentioned elements are, in my case, of visual and some of muscular type. Conventional words or other signs have to be sought for laboriously only in a secondary stage, when the mentioned associative play is sufficiently established and can be reproduced at will. . . . In a stage when words intervene at all, they are, in my case, purely auditive, but they interfere only in a secondary stage as already mentioned.

These are but a few arguments against the identity of thought and language. Clearly, one cannot *equate* thought with either speech or language. But still, language must play an important role in some cognitive processes. The processes involved in memory have often been conceptualized in terms of "verbal mediation." This is a clear area in which to begin our search for effects of language on cognition.

LANGUAGE AND MEMORY

Verbal Coding

A familiar paradigm in experimental psychology is the delayed response experiment. For example, the subject watches the experimenter hide a reward—often food—and is then required to wait for a given period of time before attempting to get the reward. Duration of delay before successful responding differs in various species. For some the longest possible delay is only a few seconds. For man, however, the delay can be indefinitely long. (In fact, with writing and other means of symbolic representation, the delay can be extended beyond living memory, as when a hunt for lost treasure is spurred by an ancient map or written clue.)

It has been found that children who have been taught verbal descriptions of the various response alternatives in an experiment rehearse the description of the cue to responding during the delay (e.g., "the peanut is under the red cup"), and in this way can retain the appropriate set to respond over a long period of time, and over various changes in the situation. Human children are thus able to bridge the time gap by means of verbal mediation. Much work of this sort has been done in both the United States (e.g., as reviewed by Spiker, 1963) and in the Soviet Union (e.g., as reviewed by Slobin, 1966b). The moral of this research is that human subjects can formulate a verbal rule which they use to guide their performance in certain types of psychological experiments, and, presumably, in corresponding types of real-life situations. Problem-solving experiments with human subjects are often different from those with animal subjects because of the use of verbal thought as a means of solution. This is, of course, in part because the solution can be easily held in memory in verbal form. But there is even more compelling evidence of the role of verbal representation in memory. What I have in mind is the fact that many memories are distorted *just because* they are stored in verbal form—because not everything can be accurately represented in a verbal summary. Verbal memory is thus a two-edged sword.

This is clearly revealed in experiments on memory for visual aspects of stimuli—e.g., form or color. Many such experiments have shown that memory of visual images can be distorted to better conform with their verbal labels (e.g., Glanzer and Clark, 1964; Lantz and Stefflre, 1964). The classic experiment in this field is a study performed in 1932 by Carmichael, Hogan, and Walter, called "An Experimental Study of the Effect of Language on the Representation of Visually Perceived Form" (1932; see also Herman, Lawless, and Marshall, 1957). These experimenters presented subjects with a set of twelve ambiguous figures, such as O-O, which could be seen as either eye-glasses or dumbells. The subjects were told that they would first see 12 figures, which they would later have to reproduce as accurately as possible. Each figure was named as it was presented—e.g., in one case the above figure was named "eye-glasses" and in the other, "dumbell." The result was that subjects tended to reproduce the ambiguous figures to better conform with their verbal labels. For example, the figure was reproduced something like OO by the first group of subjects, and something like ∞ by the second. In a task of this sort it is apparently easier for subjects to store 12 verbal labels and produce images to match these labels at a later time than it is for them to store the 12 images themselves.

Memory of real-life events, of course, is also subject to the distortions imposed by verbal encoding. This is especially evident in the case of rumor, where it is clear that verbal memory for events has changed with time, under the influence of stereotypes and expectations. This phenomenon can be reproduced in the laboratory in experiments in which a verbal description or a story is passed on from person to person, similar to the old game of "telephone." (See, for example, *Remembering* by Bartlett [1932] and *The Psychology of Rumor* by Allport and Postman [1947].) What kinds of changes take place in memory of stories or events? For one thing, there is *levelling*: many events drop out, the story becomes much shorter and schematic. But at the same time there is *sharpening*: some details achieve a peculiar sort of salience, and are repeated time after time in retelling. And finally there is *assimilation* to some schemata, or stereotypes, or expectations. To a certain extent, we remember events the way we want to; memories are often changed to match our prejudices or desires — to become more plausible or acceptable to us.

This phenomenon of schematization in memory is what George Miller refers to as *recoding* in his very important article on memory, "The magical number seven, plus or minus two" (1956). In that article Miller comes to the conclusion that one can hold no more than 7±2 "chunks" of information in immediate memory, and he discusses the cognitive economy which comes about by lumping many things together into one chunk, so to speak. Thus, for example, it may be as easy to remember a list of seven random letters as seven random words, though the seven words contain many more letters than the list of random letters. I suspect that one way of "chunking" in memory is to recode a long experience into a short description — maybe even one word — in the hope that at some future time the details can be regenerated from the memory of their brief verbal description or tag.

Why is this sort of schematization in memory necessary? A moment's thought will make the answer obvious. If you want to recall what happened yesterday, for example, and if your memory were not of this sort, you would have to relive the entire day in memory, at the same rate at which you originally lived it. Obviously, you could make no progress this way. It would take you a whole day just to remember the previous day! So it is clear that we *must* reduce our memories to the point where we can deal with a summary of some sort. Exactly how this sort of recoding is done is still pretty much of a mystery. (For some intriguing neurological suggestions see Penfield and Roberts, 1959.)

Childhood Amnesia

There are two major problems with memory—storage and retrieval. Assuming that material is somehow stored, how do you get back to it when you need it? The problem is a familiar one when trying to recall earlier experiences. Generally some verbal formulation will help you search your memory, but this convenient device seems to be of no great aid in the search for one's memories of very early childhood. Most people can't remember much of anything that happened to them before the age of two or three. Why should such memories be so elusive?

Freud believed that memories of early childhood are actually present in the adult unconscious, but inaccessible to conscious recall because they are laden with repressed matters of infantile sexuality. Could it just be "repression" which hides early memory from us, or might there be other, more cognitive reasons? Piaget (1962b) has also examined such problems, and the issue has been discussed with great insight by the psychologist Ernest Schachtel (1959). The cognitive approach to the problem reveals interesting aspects of the role played by language in memory.

Schachtel raises important objections to Freud. He points out that the Freudian explanation of repression of memories connected with infantile sexuality fails to explain why *all* memories of early childhood are so inaccessible to adult recall. Furthermore, one generally cannot bring such memories to awareness even through psychoanalysis or other means of memory stimulation.

He goes on to argue that early autobiographical memory may be impossible for strictly cognitive reasons, because:

> The categories (or schemata) for adult memory are not suitable receptacles for early childhood experiences and therefore not fit to preserve these experiences and enable their recall. The functional capacity of the conscious, adult memory is usually limited to those types of experience which the adult consciously makes and is capable of making.

What he means to say is that the child's way of perceiving the world is so different from that of the adult that the two worlds are almost mutually incomprehensible. Consider how difficult it is to imagine what a young child is really thinking and feeling—much less an infant. One reason for the difference, of course, is simply the cognitive development which takes place in the process of growing up. Another reason is tied with the fact that adults *talk* about their experiences and memories and, as we have already noted, tend to code and store their experiences linguistically. That is to say, you can get back to an adult memory by re-constructing it from a verbal description or "tag"; such verbal tags are not available for very early experiences. Schachtel points out that when you ask an adult to recount his life experiences to you, he follows certain standard "signposts" of his culture, relating such facts as education, marriage, jobs, trips, and so on. These memories are schematic, and generally do not have the vividness or force of living experience. Living and telling are two different modes, and only the skilled writer or story-teller can breathe life into a retrospective account. (In reports of drug experiences the point is often made that the experience cannot be conveyed verbally; but note that this is true also of everyday experiences.)

Before returning to the problem of childhood amnesia, it is worth examining the effect of verbal re-telling of life experience. Sartre, in his novel *Nausea* (1959, pp. 56–58), lucidly expresses the dilemma posed by these two modes of living or remembering—the experiential versus the symbolic or "told":

> This is what I thought: for the most banal event to become an adventure, you must (and this is enough) begin to recount it. This is what fools people: a man is always a teller of tales, he lives surrounded by his stories and the stories of others, he sees everything that happens to him through them; and he tries to live his own life as if he were telling a story.
>
> But you have to choose: live or tell. For example, when I was in Hamburg, with that Erna girl I didn't trust and who was afraid of me, I led a funny sort of life. But I was in the middle of it, I didn't think about it. And then one evening, in a little café in San Pauli, she left me to go to the ladies' room. I stayed alone, there was a phonograph playing "Blue Skies." I began to tell myself what had happened since I landed. . . . Then I felt violently that I was having an adventure. But Erna came back and sat down beside me, she wound her arms around my neck and I hated her without knowing why. I understand now: one had to begin living again and the adventure was fading out.
>
> Nothing happens while you live. The scenery changes, people come in and go out, that's all. There are no beginnings. Days are tacked on to days without rhyme or reason, an interminable, monotonous addition. . . .
>
> That's living. But everything changes when you tell about life; it's a change no one notices: the proof is that people talk about true stories. As if there could possibly be true stories; things hap-

pen one way and we tell about them in the opposite sense. You seem to start at the beginning: "It was a fine autumn evening in 1922. I was a notary's clerk in Marommes." And in reality you have started at the end. It was there, invisible and present, it is the one which gives to words the pomp and value of a beginning. "I was out walking, I had left the town without realizing it, I was thinking about my money troubles." This sentence, taken simply for what it is, means that the man was absorbed, morose, a hundred leagues from an adventure, exactly in the mood to let things happen without noticing them. But the end is there, transforming everything. For us, the man is already the hero of the story. His moroseness, his money troubles are much more precious than ours, they are all gilded by the light of future passions. And the story goes on in the reverse: instants have stopped piling themselves up in a lighthearted way one on top of the other, they are snapped up by the end of the story which draws them and each one of them in turn, draws out the preceding instant: "It was night, the street was deserted." The phrase is cast out negligently, it seems superfluous; but we do not let ourselves be caught and we put it aside: this is a piece of information whose value we shall subsequently appreciate. And we feel that the hero has lived all the details of this night like annunciations, promises, or even that he lived only those that were promises, blind and deaf to all that did not herald adventure. We forget that the future was not yet there; the man was walking in a night without forethought, a night which offered him a choice of dull rich prizes, and he did not make his choice.

I wanted the moments of my life to follow and order themselves like those of a life remembered. You might as well try and catch time by the tail.

We can bring this whole compelling train of thought back to the problem of childhood amnesia. In this regard, Schachtel makes two major points: (1) The child has no schemata, no internal interpretive framework, for the preservation of his very earliest memories. (2) Those schemata which he learns later in childhood are not appropriate for the interpretation or re-coding of his early experience.

How can we imagine what the world looks like to a child before he has developed the concepts such as object permanence or conservation of quantity? As he grows bigger, objects change in relative size for the child, and, at the same time, they are being labelled, organized, grouped, and regrouped into new categories on the basis of the language he is learning.

There is also another important way in which childhood experience differs from adult experience. At first the child relies most heavily on the *proximity senses* (smell, taste, touch), and only later do the *distance senses* (sight, hearing) become the dominant ones. We have an inadequate vocabulary for expressing sensations of the proximity senses. Furthermore, such sensations are often taboo, and seem to arouse more intense pleasure and disgust than sensations of the distance receptors. The child learns a well-developed vocabulary to deal with experiences of sight and sound, but these do not help him record his early experiences in a manner which is available to retrieval.

So it would seem that most of the child's early memories are connected with stimuli no longer available to him—stimuli of the proximity senses, stimuli falling into categories different from the ones learned later in life, and stimuli seen from a different vantage point from that used by the adult. No wonder Proust found it necessary to assume certain body postures, or find certain odors, and so on, in order to revive early memories in his "recherche du temps perdu"—in his "remembrance of times past."

To summarize Schachtel's argument in a sentence, then: One's memory of early childhood experiences may be not so much willfully repressed as simply inaccessible to recall, though not forgotten.

We have, however, a variety of ways of representing experiences to ourselves; language is only one—though a very useful one in many cases. It is depressing that our earliest experiences are generally irretrievable without special means. But what about our earliest actual memories—memories which consist of visual images and sensations, but which are accessible by means of a linkage to some verbal cue. I'm afraid that even here—with graphic memories of our own experiences—we can never be sure how much the image has been affected by the verbal encoding. As a most extreme example of the interaction of different means of representation in memory, consider the following reminiscence of Jean Piaget (1962b, pp. 187–188):

> There is also the question of memories which depend on other people. For instance, one of my first memories would date, if it were true, from my second year. I can still see, most clearly, the following scene, in which I believed until I was about fifteen. I was sitting in my pram, which my nurse was pushing in the Champs Elysées, when a man tried to kidnap me. I was held in by the strap fastened round me while my nurse bravely tried to stand between me and the thief. She received various scratches, and I can still see vaguely those on her face. Then a crowd gathered, a policeman with a short cloak and a white baton came up, and the

man took to his heels. I can still see the whole scene, and can even place it near the tube station. When I was about fifteen, my parents received a letter from my former nurse saying that she had been converted to the Salvation Army. She wanted to confess her past faults, and in particular to return the watch she had been given as a reward on this occasion. She had made up the whole story, faking the scratches. I therefore must have heard, as a child, the account of this story, which my parents believed, and projected it into the past in the form of a visual memory, which was a memory of a memory, but false. Many real memories are doubtless of the same order.

Under conditions such as these, it is very hard indeed to ever fully carry out the ancient advice, "Know thyself!" It is rather like reading the newspapers — you have to take on faith that there is some correspondence between the events and their reporting — and you know how hazardous that can be.

LANGUAGE AND COGNITIVE DEVELOPMENT

It should be clear by now that language does not embrace all of cognition, but we have yet to explore fully the degree and nature of the role played by language. Language is one of several means of representation. Taking this last term quite literally, we see that we are concerned with re-presentation, that is, the problem of presenting ourselves with experience again at some later time. As in the discussion of memory, the matter is one of internal coding of experience. The psychologist Jerome Bruner (1966) has pointed to two other major modes of representation, contrasting them with linguistic representation.

A primitive but often useful means of representation is through action. Some things are best demonstrated by doing — as, for example, using tools, tying knots, and other motor skills. Probably many things we know how to do are represented by some sort of muscle imagery. Children learn much about the world through active manipulation, and there is a good deal of evidence that "enactive" representation is an early means for representing objects.

Enactive representation is limited, however, in that it is sequentially ordered and not easily reversible. If you learn your way from home to work by remembering a series of left and right turns, you will have difficulty in finding yourself if you get lost, for you have no overall representation of the route. If you have a map (or a visual image) of the route, however, you can scan it back and forth and find your place and your way. Thus there is another, more compact mode of representation which uses visual imagery as its mode. This mode allows for action-free representation.

The most supple mode of action-free representation, however, is language (and the other symbolic systems invented by man, such as mathematical systems). Systems such as language make it possible to invent new symbols to represent anything—even things which cannot be felt or seen. And, given rules of combination and recombination, such as grammar, we can deal with all manner of possibilities, going far beyond things and events we have experienced directly.

Thus there are at least three major means available for representing experience: action, imagery, and language. No one mode serves all human purposes: we must learn manipulative skills, visual configurations, social customs, science, history, and so on. The three modes are used separately and in interaction. Furthermore, as discussed above, there must be inarticulate forms of thought which precede the production of acts, images, or utterances.

Bruner, Piaget, and others have presented evidence that the modes of representation develop in the order in which we have discussed them. We do not have the means here to evaluate this complex issue, but a few examples may be illuminating. As for the enactive mode, Piaget provides us with valuable observations from his own children during their first year of life (1954). At first it seems that objects are, to a great extent, represented in terms of action. Consider the following example, taken from Piaget's observations of his seven-month-old son (p. 22):

> Laurent . . . loses a cigarette box which he has just grasped and swung to and fro. Unintentionally he drops it outside the visual field. He then immediately brings his hand before his eyes and looks at it for a long time with an expression of surprise, disappointment, something like an expression of its disappearance. But far from considering the loss as irremediable, he begins again to swing his hand, although it is empty. After this he looks at it once more! For anyone who has seen this act and the child's expression, it is impossible not to interpret such behavior as an attempt to make the object come back. Such an observation . . . places in full light the true *nature of the object peculiar to this stage: a mere extension of the action.*

Several months later, action and object are not so closely tied. Earlier, the child would not show signs of missing an object when it was removed—unless he had already begun reaching for it. But later he will cry and search for an object which is presented for a moment and then hidden, even if he had not begun to reach for it. He no longer repeats a movement to restore the object, but seems to have an inner image of it. Development seems to go from a direct momentary prehensive definition of an object to a definition which is increasingly less reliant on action and more reliant upon visual representation (although certain basic characteristics of visual representation are, of course, built-in at birth).

With age, visual imagery seems to play a more and more important role. There is a considerable literature on children's use of imagery. This literature points to interesting conclusions about differences between children and adults in use of imagery: (1) Children use *more imagery* in carrying out intellectual tasks; (2) their imagery is more *particularistic*, rather than generic and schematic; and (3) children's images seem to have *greater vividness and detail*.

In the book, *Studies in Cognitive Growth* (1966), Bruner and his co-workers report a number of studies carried out at the Harvard Center for Cognitive Studies documenting the use of imagery by children in intellectual tasks, and the shift with age from visual to linguistic means of dealing with these tasks. For example, if children are given a collection of pictures to be sorted into categories, the younger children sort on the basis of visual features, such as color, size, pattern, and so on, while the older children sort on the basis of some superordinate linguistic concept. A six-year-old may group together *boat, ruler, doll, bicycle, scissors, saw, shoe, gloves, barn, candle, pie, nails, taxi* because: "Some are red, some are gold, and some are yellow. One is white, some are brown, and some are blue." Or he may group together *screw, ruler, nails, candle, hammer, taxi, coat, scissors, sword, bicycle* because: "They have a part that you get dressed with, or they have holes in them, or you use them for tools, taxi goes with bicycle." By age eight the picture is different. Bruner reports: "Increasingly with development the child isolates one or more attributes that are common to all the items in the group: 'They are all tools,' or 'You can eat with them,' or 'They can all move,' and so on" (1966, pp. 83–84). The child may be so struck by vivid perceptual details which attract him from moment to moment that he is prevented from discerning common features. Bruner suggests that the growth of linguistic skills gradually allows the child to code and compare attributes of objects verbally, thus freeing him from the momentary perceptual impact of one attribute or another.

The picture is not as simple as this, however. Note that both six- and eight-year-olds have well-developed linguistic systems, but their means for sorting pictures into categories are quite different. Simply having language is not enough: something else must change with growth. The old "nature-nurture" debate rages strongly in this domain, and we are far from clear answers. The Americans and the Russians tend to stress the role of training and instruction in cognitive development; whereas Piaget and his school stress the role of naturally-developing cognitive growth as the child interacts with his environment. Bruner's book suggests that children must be trained – chiefly through formal school instruction – to use language in ways which free them from attending to concrete, perceptual attributes of things. In regard to the picture-sorting task, for example, he says that the shift from the use of perceptual cues to more abstract, superordinate grouping criteria "is *not* a universal property of 'growing up'" (1966, p. 85). A number of the experiments in *Studies in Cognitive Growth* were carried out in a variety of cultural settings, leading to the conclusion that

> the "natural" terminus of growth depends to a very considerable extent on the pattern imposed by the culture. The techniques used [here] have, in modified form, been used in studies of children in Alaska, Mexico, and Senegal . . . and it is plain that school children in Dakar or Mexico City look very much like the school children of [suburban Boston]. But it is equally plain that the village child of rural Mexico and the unschooled Wolof of Senegal seem very different . . . much more perceptually oriented (Bruner et al., 1966, p. 85).

Bruner et al. thus suggest that the school is a very important determiner of the use of language to facilitate cognitive growth. In school children must learn to use language in the absence of immediate context. This is true especially of learning to read and write, but it applies to a broader range of linguistic tasks which a child must learn to perform in a school setting. Bruner's cross-cultural studies suggest that the sort of intellectual training a child receives is more important than the particular language he happens to speak – as far as the general course of his cognitive growth is concerned.

A similar argument has been developed in the provocative work of the British sociologist Basil Bernstein. He distinguishes between uses of language which are "context bound" ("restricted codes") and uses which are more free of immediate nonlinguistic context. Context independent use of language ("elaborated codes") is necessary when communicating with people who do not share the knowledge and assumptions of the speaker. In a recent unpublished paper, "A Critique of the Concept 'Compensatory Education,'" Bernstein gives a graphic example in which he presents these two uses of language as broadly characteristic of sociolinguistic differences between British middle-class and working-class children:

Consider, for example, the two following stories which Peter Hawkins . . . constructed as a result of his analysis of the speech of middle-class and working-class five-year old children. The children were given a series of four pictures which told a story and then were invited to tell the story. The first picture shows some boys playing football, in the second the ball goes through the window of a house, the third shows a woman looking out of the window and in the fourth the children are moving away. Here are the two stories:

> (1) Three boys are playing football and one boy kicks the ball and it goes through the window   the ball breaks the window   and the boys are looking at it   and a man comes out and shouts at them   because they've broken the window   so they run away   and then that lady looks out of her window   and she tells the boys off.

No. of nouns: 13   No. of pronouns: 6

> (2) They're playing football   and he kicks it and it goes through there   it breaks the window and they're looking at it   and he comes out   and shouts at them because they've broken it   so they run away   and then she looks out   and she tells them off.

No. of nouns: 2   No. of pronouns: 14

With the first story the reader does not have to have the four pictures which were used as the basis for the story, whereas in the case of the second story the reader would require the initial pictures in order to make sense of the story. The first story is free of the context which generated it, whereas the second story is much more closely tied to the context.

Here we have an excellent statement of the sort of context-free, or elaborated use of language which is called for in formal schooling. Bernstein has developed these notions in an important sociolinguistic theory, in which factors of communication and control in child-rearing and schooling play an important role in developing the child's use of language. (For a recent and lucid exposition of this theory, see Bernstein's paper in Gumperz and Hymes [in press].)

Another important consequence of the use of language is that the child does not have to perform direct tests to acquire knowledge. By dealing with a problem verbally, he can act on *possible information* in addition to actual information—that is, he can eliminate possibilities through rea-

Reprinted from *Directions in Sociolinguistics* edited by J. J. Gumperz and D. Hymes, by permission of Holt, Rinehart and Winston, Inc., Chaucer Publishing Co. Ltd., and Basil Bernstein.

soning, and can devise intelligent tests of a situation to replace random probing or trial-and-error.

We still do not have sufficient information, however, to determine the extent to which such reasoning abilities require language or schooling. We must know much more about the level of intellectual development reached by individuals deprived of language or deprived of formal education. The work of Piaget's school strongly suggests that language more often *reflects* than *determines* cognitive development. He and his colleagues have made careful attempts to train children in problem solving by teaching them new ways of talking about particular tasks and concepts. (See Inhelder et al., 1966.) The general finding has been that special linguistic training will be of no avail to a child unless his level of cognitive development has already reached the point at which it can embrace the relevant concepts represented by the words. The results of concerted linguistic training on certain tasks ("conservation tasks," as referred to below) led the Piagetians to the following careful and plausible conclusion (Inhelder et al., 1966, p. 163):

> Our general systematic conclusions with respect to the effects of language are straightforward. First, language training, among other types of training, operates to direct the child's interactions with the environment and thus to "focus" on relevant dimensions of task situations. Second, the observed changes in the justifications given [by children] for answers in the conservation task suggest that language does aid in the storage and retrieval of relevant information. However, our evidence offers little, if any, support for the contention that language learning per se contributes to the *integration and coordination* of "informational units" necessary for the achievement of the conservation concepts.
>
> Language learning does not provide, in our opinion, a ready-made "lattice" or lens which organizes the child's perceptual world. Rather, the lattice is constructed in the process of the development of intelligence, i.e., through the actions of the child on the environment and the interiorization of these actions to form operational structures. This does not imply that language plays no role in the refinements and adjustments of the "lattice" to conform to cultural-social-linguistic normative patterns. Nor do we intend to exclude the possibility of feedback of language on operational structures directly, particularly at the level of logical-operational thought where in many cases the reasoning processes may be more closely linked to language. . . . The magnitude of the effects [of language upon cognition] appear dependent on the perceptual components of the task, the developmental level of the

child, and the type of thought operations necessary for solution of the task.

The Piagetian experiments raise a number of important points. For one, note the emphasis on interiorization of actions to form "operational structures." More simply stated, the child acts upon the world and builds internal models of the nature of reality on the basis of these actions and their results. Such interaction with the environment, of course, need not be solely verbal.

Note also that language training alone is not sufficient to move a child from one developmental stage to the next. Language training here, however, is in a limited experimental situation, and is not as all-pervasive as the sort of training which occurs in the process of formal schooling. It is this sort of linguistic training which Bruner and his co-workers stress in their book, when noting differences between peasant and urban children, and between schooled and unschooled children in various cultures. In the context of formal education, however, it is difficult to separate the role of language per se from the entire range of experience and special training involved in going to school. The questions are far from closed, although the Harvard and Geneva projects offer—and will no doubt continue to offer—intriguing and suggestive leads.

Another very important line of evidence in regard to the role of language in cognitive development comes from the study of deaf children. Because such children lack verbal language and have a more limited educational experience, they offer a significant control group to the normal children we have considered thus far. If their cognitive development does not differ markedly from that of normal children, we will have important support for Piaget's emphasis on the primacy of cognitive maturation, guided by various sorts of experience. The central question here is whether the possession of language is an essential determiner of the stages of cognitive development observed by Piaget and others, or whether language just provides experiences which help make this development possible. If the latter is more nearly true, then maybe the experience of living itself, in the absence of language, will also move a child forward in cognitive development. These propositions can be tested —to some extent—by studying the cognitive development of deaf children, who have very little language at all—usually no language (in our sense of verbal language) in the formative years.

This line of research has been most widely developed by Hans Furth and his co-workers at the Catholic University in Washington, D.C., and is summarized in a book entitled *Thinking Without Language: Psychological Implications of Deafness* (1966). Furth reports that most American deaf children do not learn English—written or spoken—until rather late in life, and that in most cases it is never adequately acquired. In fact, Furth claims that it remains almost a foreign language for most American deaf people. Those deaf children who have deaf parents learn the gestural sign language, normally and easily, just like any other native language. But for most deaf children there is no early exposure to sign language, and Furth criticizes the policy of most American schools for the deaf to withhold sign language from deaf children in the hope that they will learn English instead. This unfortunate situation has set up the conditions for a "natural experiment" in which the cognitive development of children who are grossly language deficient can be compared with that of normal children. Furth reports a large number of studies of this sort, most of them pointing to the striking conclusion that deaf children are not drastically different from hearing children in intellectual performance. The course of cognitive development in both cases follows the same basic stages, though in some instances the rate of development may be slower for the deaf. It is quite likely, though, that this occasional slowness may be due not so much to specific lack of language as to general lack of experience, given the sort of environment in which many deaf children are raised. In Furth's studies of deaf and hearing adults he finds no significant differences in basic cognitive abilities, though most of his deaf subjects could barely read and write or speak English.

As the title of Furth's book suggests, perhaps language is not as important as we thought after all. He concludes (1964, p. 160):

> By generalizing the results of the studies summarized above and applying them to a theoretical position on the influence of language on intellective development, the following is suggested: (a) Language does not influence intellectual development in any direct, general, or decisive way. (b) The influence of language may be indirect or specific and may accelerate intellectual development: by providing the opportunity for additional experience through giving information and exchange of ideas and by furnishing ready symbols (words) and linguistic habits in specific situations.
>
> From this position it should follow that persons deficient in linguistic experience or skill (a) are not permanently or generally retarded in intellectual ability, but (b) may be temporarily retarded during their developmental phase because of lack of sufficient general experience and (c) they may be retarded on certain specific tasks in which available word symbols or linguistic habits facilitate solution.

It seems that this summary points to the sort of conclusion which psychology will eventually have to reach—though, of course, in more detail. Language clearly plays some role in some aspects of cognition and cognitive development. The task remaining before us is to characterize the varying roles played by language in varying forms of cognitive functioning.

Furth's work underlines the importance of language in communication between people: " . . . deaf children are bound to be deficient in many ordinary experiences and occasions which motivate other children to ask questions, reason, and organize mentally. . . . this experiential deficiency is directly related to linguistic deficiency, or more accurately, to the prevailing lack of ordinary communication."

Vygotsky and Piaget have also devoted special attention to the role played by communication with others in the development of thought. Vygotsky formulated the basic problem in the following terms, as one of investigating "how a function, arising in communication and at first divided between two people, can restructure all of the activity of the child and gradually change into the complicated mediated functional system which characterizes the structure of his mental processes" (Luria, 1959, p. 524). The impetus for Vygotsky's work was Piaget's first book, *The Language and Thought of the Child* (1923). In this work Piaget distinguished between "egocentric" and "socialized speech," and portrayed development as a transition from one to the other. In egocentric speech, the child

> does not bother to know to whom he is speaking nor whether he is being listened to. He talks either for himself or for the pleasure of associating anyone who happens to be there with the activity of the moment. This talk is egocentric . . . chiefly because he does not attempt to place himself at the point of view of his hearer. . . . The child asks for no more than apparent interest, though he has the illusion . . . of being heard and understood (Piaget, 1955, p. 32).

Egocentric speech, for Piaget, is eventually replaced by socialized speech, which takes account of the point of view of the listener and makes true dialogue possible. Piaget was concerned mainly with the development of thought in the child, and assigned no special functions to egocentric speech, attributing it to early "verbal incontinence."

Vygotsky, on the other hand, stressed that all speech is social in origin, and sought to discover the functions served by early overt speech in the life of the child. He opposed both Piaget's notion of the eventual atrophy of egocentric "outer speech" and Watson's position that this speech, under the pressure not to talk out loud, was simply internalized to become subvocal speech, and thus the equivalent of thought. Rather, he attempted to show that early egocentric speech splits from communicative speech, and is a transition stage between full-fledged speech out loud and silent thought. In the process, egocentric speech becomes more and more abbreviated and idiosyncratic, eventually becoming inner speech, or verbal thought, qualitatively different from outer speech. In a series of ingenious experiments Vygotsky and his co-workers in Moscow set out to show that the egocentric speech of the young child serves a useful function in his mental development, and that he does try and in fact wants to communicate with others, though at first he cannot well differentiate "speech for oneself" from "speech for others."

In one series of experiments they sought to demonstrate that the spontaneous speech of children serves a practical function, not only accompanying activity, but serving to orient it. For example, a child whose crayon broke while he was drawing said the word "broken" out loud, and then went on to draw a broken car. They also found that spontaneous speech increased markedly when a child was faced with problem situations, and in situations where frustrations were introduced. In other experiments, spontaneous speech seemed to be used to orient and guide the child's activity. Such findings led Vygotsky to propose that the use of speech in such situations facilitates the understanding of the problem, and that speech, even in early years, serves an adaptive planning function in the life of the child.

In other experiments, Vygotsky demonstrated that the child's speech is communicative in its aim. For example, when a child was placed in a group of deaf-and-dumb children, or children speaking a foreign language, or even in a very noisy environment, his own spontaneous speech dropped to almost nothing.

Finally, Vygotsky found that egocentric speech becomes less and less intelligible from three to seven years of age, finally disappearing on an overt level, thus supporting his notion that egocentric speech is on its way to becoming inner speech. He concludes (1962):

> We consider that the total development runs as follows: The primary function of speech, in both children and adults, is communication, social contact. The earliest speech of the child is therefore essentially social. . . . At a certain age the social speech of the child is quite sharply divided into egocentric and communicative speech (p. 19).
>
> Our experimental results indicate that the function of egocentric speech is similar to that of inner speech: It does not merely accompany the child's activity; it serves mental orientation, conscious understanding; it helps in overcoming difficulties; it is speech for oneself, intimately and usefully connected with the child's thinking. . . . In the end, it becomes inner speech (p. 133).

These experimental findings and conclusions have recently received significant support in this country in the work of Kohlberg and his colleagues (1968). And Piaget himself, who has long outlived Vygotsky, has clearly expressed similar views on the role of communication with others in aiding cognitive development. This is especially clear in his reply to the 1962 English translation of Vygotsky's *Thought and Language* — unfortunately Piaget's first reading of Vygotsky's great work of 1934. In his reply, Piaget essentially agrees with the outlines of Vygotsky's notion of the role of inner speech, and goes on to discuss the role of communication (1962a):

> I have used the term egocentrism to designate the initial inability to decenter, to shift the cognitive perspective. . . . Cognitive egocentrism . . . stems from a lack of differentiation between one's own point of view and the other possible ones, and not at all from an individualism that precedes relations with others. . . .
>
> . . . [Vygotsky] proposed a new hypothesis: that egocentric speech is the point of departure for the development of inner speech, which is found at a later stage of development, and that this interiorized language can serve both autistic ends and logical thinking. I find myself in complete agreement with these hypotheses.
>
> . . . In egocentric speech the child speaks according to himself. [This is] the only valid meaning of egocentrism: the lack of decentering, of the ability to shift mental perspective, in social relationships as well as in others. Moreover, I think that it is precisely cooperation with others (on the cognitive plane) that teaches us to speak according to others and not simply from our own point of view.

This last point is especially important: Piaget sees this inability to "decenter" as a general cognitive phenomenon, from which the child frees himself, in part, through communication with others (though not necessarily *only* linguistic communication). He implies that the ability to communicate adequately is closely bound up with cognitive development in general.

The question of the role of communicative speech in cognitive development provides a perspective from which to view the work of Bruner, Bernstein, Furth, Vygotsky, and Piaget. In *Studies in Cognitive Growth*, Bruner discusses five possible sources of language-influenced intellectual development: (1) Words can serve as "invitations to form concepts." That is, the very occurrence of unfamiliar words stimulates the child to discover the meanings of those words. (2) Dialogue between adult and child can serve to orient and educate the child, providing an important source of experience and knowledge. (3) School creates the need for new uses of language—particularly context-free and elaborated uses. (4) Scientific concepts are developed in a culture and are conveyed verbally. (5) The occurrence of conflict between modes of representation can be a source of intellectual development.

We have touched upon these major issues briefly. These five aspects of language use in cognitive development vary with culture and social class, interact with one another, and can influence intelligence in many ways. Given these multifarious questions about the role of language in human behavior, we must, of course, accept the platitude that language is an important component of the psychological nature of man. But we are still a long way from understanding the specific aspects and functions of this component in all of human behavior and cognition.

In concluding, let us touch on one more aspect of the problem—a very intriguing aspect: Given that language has effects such as those discussed above, does it make any difference which particular human language an individual happens to speak?

LINGUISTIC RELATIVITY AND DETERMINISM

The notion that different languages influence thinking in different ways has been present since the beginning of philosophy. In American social science this hypothesis of *linguistic relativity and determinism* has come to bear the name of the "Whorfian hypothesis," after the linguist Benjamin Lee Whorf who devoted great attention to the problem (Whorf, 1956). Let us begin with an early statement of the problem by Edward Sapir, the great linguist who was Whorf's teacher (in Mandelbaun, 1958, p. 162).

> Human beings do not live in the objective world alone, nor alone in the world of social activity as ordinarily understood, but are very much at the mercy of the particular language which has become the medium of expression for their society. It is quite an illusion to imagine that one adjusts to reality essentially without the use of language and that language is merely an incidental means of solving specific problems of communication or reflection. The fact of the matter is that the "real world" is to a large extent unconsciously built up on the language habits of the group. . . . We see and hear and otherwise experience very largely as we do because the language habits of our community predispose certain choices of interpretation.

The statement raises several important points. Sapir holds that *all* of experience is influenced by the particular language one speaks. (We are not told what aspects of language are relevant.) The strength of this influence is not clear: earlier he says we are "at the mercy of language"; later he simply says that "the language habits . . . predispose certain choices of interpretation." The earlier statement is quite strong, while the later, weaker, statement can be accomodated to the arguments developed earlier in this chapter. It is also clear from the statement that different languages are held to have different effects on thought and experience. Sapir's statement thus advances the notions of *linguistic determinism* (language can determine cognition) and *linguistic relativity* (the determinism is relative to the particular language spoken), in both a strong and weak version. These notions must be examined more carefully.

First of all, why should one even expect there to be language-specific effects on cognition—that is, what sort of evidence impels one to postulate linguistic relativity? Students are often struck by the apparent strangeness of foreign languages, especially when the language is not closely related to the native language. People begin to think about linguistic relativity when they compare languages and discover how different the categories of experience embodied in various languages can be. Categories can be represented in various ways by language: (1) by individual words in the lexicon (*house, white*, etc.), (2) also by parts of words which perform grammatical functions (*house* vs. *houses* vs. *house's; white* vs. *whiter* vs. *whiten* vs. *whiteness*; etc.), and (3) also by a variety of grammatical processes (e.g., word order as used to distinguish subject and object in English: *The man hit the ball* vs. *The ball hit the man*). As you will see shortly, languages differ greatly both in the categories they express and the particular linguistic means used for the representation of given categories. These differences go deeper than the well-known fact that most words have no completely perfect translation equivalent from one language to another, for you will note from the above English examples that categories can be expressed both *lexically* and *grammatically*. We'll go into this distinction in more detail in a moment. But first let me point out why we have to specify what sorts of differences between languages we want to deal with in trying to connect linguistic with nonlinguistic phenomena.

The specification of differences is the first of three problems which must be considered in trying to relate these two sorts of phenomena. The first question asks: (1) *What kinds of linguistic facts are being referred to?* Are we concerned with whether a language has a term for a specific concept, or whether a concept is embodied in an obligatory grammatical distinction, and so on.

Of course, there is a necessary second question: (2) *With what kinds of phenomena is a connection being made?* For example, do we want to relate the linguistic facts we have discovered with facts of sense perception, or memory, or cultural behavior, or what? Whorf was most interested in relating both the lexicon and the grammar—especially the grammar—to the total *Weltanschauung*, the total world view of a culture. His was the most pervasive sort of equation proposed, and so his approach is sometimes called the "language-Weltanschauung hypothesis."

And finally we must also ask: (3) *What is the nature of the connection?* Is it a causal relation—and, if so, which is the causal factor, the linguistic or the nonlinguistic? Most of the provocative theorizing on this matter assumes that the language in some way determines other behaviors, rather than the other way around. And there are two broad types of theories here, frequently referred to as the "strong" and the "weak" versions of the Whorf hypothesis. The strong form—often espoused by Whorf himself—holds that the language *determines* thought and behavior patterns; that the language is a sort of mold for thought and philosophy. The weak form—usually held to today in one way or another—merely asserts that certain aspects of language can predispose people to think or act in one way rather than another, but that there is no rigid determinism: One is not fully a prisoner of one's language; it is just a guide to thought and other sorts of behavior.

Thus we have a two-way classification, in which one looks either to the lexicon or the grammar, and posits either a strong or a weak relation between an aspect of language and aspects of thought or action. There are accordingly at least four forms of the linguistic relativity and determinism hypothesis, fitting into the four cells of the following table:

| | | *Linguistic Variables* | |
		Lexical	Grammatical
Form of Determinism	Strong		
	Weak		

·I think there are also other confusions in regard to the causal question. Clearly the case must be different for the history of a *culture* and the history of an *individual.* As Sapir pointed out so well (1912), cultural phenomena must, in very early times, have determined certain linguistic forms; but culture changes much more quickly than language, and so many archaisms, from a cultural-determinism point of view, are found in every language. In this sense, then, the language, and not the cultural behavior, is seen as the dependent variable. But this is an historical question. As far as any individual is concerned, he is born into an existing cultural and linguistic community, and both cultural and linguistic forms influence his cognitive development.

Finally, Sapir also points out another sort of causal relation—one in which both the linguistic forms and the cultural forms are determined by a third factor, for example, the topography of the geographical area in which a society dwells. He speaks (1912) of the Paiute Indians, who live in the desert and are faced with the need of finding water. Their language allows them to describe topological features in great detail. Here is a case where environment determines both the linguistic and the cultural concern with the topology of the terrain.

I think it is very important to bear these three questions in mind: the nature of the linguistic evidence, the nature of the behavioral evidence, and the causal nature of the connection. Most of the early philosophers and linguists concerned with linguistic relativity and determinism failed to spell out the second and third questions carefully, and often spoke as if a linguistic difference necessarily implied a cognitive difference, without presenting further evidence. Only a few psychological experiments in recent years have tried to relate *specific* linguistic differences to *specific* sorts of behavior—and even when a relation *is* found, it is not clear just what the causal nature of the relation is. (Much of this work is summarized in Lenneberg, 1967.)

Let us now take up these questions in more detail. First of all, what sorts of evidence have brought people to talk about linguistic relativity at all? We can begin with the lexical level—the matter of what words are found in a given language, and what they refer to. (This discussion follows, in part, Fishman's "systematization of the Whorfian hypothesis" [1960].)

When you compare two languages, you may find that one of them has a word for which there is no one-word equivalent at all in the other language. For example, there is no one-word English equivalent for the German *Gemütlichkeit*. (But note that this does not prevent us from learning what the German term means, and borrowing it for use in English. We have thousands of words which we have borrowed from other languages whenever necessary. I think it could only be argued, in this regard, that the Germans may be more sensitive to the attribute of *Gemütlichkeit*—but this would be a very difficult sort of nonlinguistic behavior to measure. Note also that when new concepts arise, we invent new words to refer to them: "hippie," "de-escalation," and on and on.)

Languages also differ in providing superordinate terms to name various categories. For example, English has the superordinates *animal*, *bird*, *insect*, and *creature*, which some languages lack; but, on the other hand, we don't have a superordinate term for "fruit and nuts," while the

Chinese do. (I think that this sort of evidence can only be used in regard to the weak form of the hypothesis; we can certainly conceive of grouping fruit and nuts together—though we may not ordinarily do so; and we can use the productive aspects of our language to form an expression such as "fruit and nuts" when a single word is lacking.) Similarly, the Arabs are said to have many terms for various breeds of horses, but no superordinate term for horses in general; the Aztecs had one word for snow, ice, and cold, where we have several and the Eskimos have even more, and so on, ad infinitum. Such evidence was adduced by the volumes of German philologists of the nineteenth century, and served as grist for the mills of those philosophers who wanted to show that other peoples thought in distinctly different ways (generally inferior) from "modern Europeans."

Languages also differ lexically in the ways in which they divide various semantic domains. One of the most popular areas of investigation in this regard is the color continuum, since it is so objectively definable, and since it has no natural boundaries. Languages differ in the number and types of cuts they make on this continuum. Gleason, for example, presents the following comparison of divisions of the spectrum by speakers of English, Shona (spoken in Rhodesia), and Bassa (Liberia) (1961, p. 4):

ENGLISH

purple	blue	green	yel-low	orange	red

SHONA

cips^{w}uka	citema	cicena	cips^{w}uka

BASSA

hui	ziza

A comparison of the above three continua draws out some significant points. Consider, for example, a color which we would label "greenish-yellow." Such a color is designated by a compound word in English because it lies on the border between two color categories. If you measure subjects' response times in naming color chips, you find that it takes longer to name a borderline color (like greenish-yellow) than a "pure" color. A pure color comes from the center of a named category, and is labelled with a single word (e.g., "yellow," "green"). However, an uncertain "greenish-yellow" or "yellowish-green" color chip may be quickly and easily labelled by a speaker of Shona, who would see it as a pure *cicena*. Each semantic system carries with it the implication that a given stimulus event will be the best exemplar of a named category, and that naming difficulties will occur at the boundaries between named categories.

Likewise, research (summarized in Lenneberg, 1967) has shown that color labels can influence memory for color, in consonance with our earlier discussion of language and memory. For example, a slightly off-green may be remembered as green, because there is no way of easily coding "slightly off-green" for later color recognition.

Another frequently-cited example of different divisions of a domain is Whorf's example (1956) of the Eskimos, who have more words for snow than we do. Note, though, that in all such cases it is the presence or absence of a *single* word which is offered as evidence for linguistic relativity and determinism. As I pointed out above, every language makes it possible to *combine* words productively; indeed, Whorf could not have explained the Eskimo distinctions without recourse to the English means of forming phrases and sentences. Roger Brown (1958) has discussed these matters in terms of the problem of *codability*—that is, the ease with which a concept can be encoded in a given language. To speak of ease of codability, however, clearly returns us to the weak form of the Whorfian hypothesis: in some languages it may be *easier* for speakers to think or talk about certain things because their language makes it easy for them to do so.

The problem throughout is one of clearly demonstrating the effect of codability on some other behavior. Let me give you another example here that is frequently cited: In some languages certain words have additional shades or ranges of meaning than their cognates or best equivalents in other languages. In French one term, *conscience*, is used for the two English terms, *conscience* and *consciousness*. On the one hand, this means that French speakers do not have as easily available to them a distinction that we have. On the other hand, it means that they have more easily available to them a partial identity of these two terms which is very difficult for us to fully appreciate. Some people think it possible to demonstrate that this linguistic identity has led to a greater conceptual fusion for French thinkers between the concepts of "conscience" and "consciousness" than has been true for English or German thinkers.

Lexical differences between languages can be characterized in terms of the three sorts of differences just considered: missing terms, missing superordinates, and different divisions of domains. The major issue here seems to hinge on the relative codability of concepts. Although it is a debatable point, I would tend to believe that any concept can somehow be encoded in any language, though with ease in some, and by complex circumlocutions in others. Thus, in regard to the lexical level, I would favor the weak form of the Whorfian hypothesis. This form draws an important distinction between *habitual* and *potential* behavior. For example, although all men can potentially discriminate a huge number of colors, most people use but a few habitual color terms in everyday speech. While it may be true that, with some effort, one could say anything in any language, we tend to say things which can be fairly conveniently encoded, and we frequently assimilate experience to the categories of the linguistic code. Thus a list of frequently-occurring words in a given language community will give you a good preliminary index of what is probably of special importance to the members of that group. Other things can, of course, be conveyed by more complex utterances, but this is not economical for important discriminations.

Now what about the *grammatical* level? Here I think the question of determinism becomes quite intriguing, because there is a variety of obligatory classifications embodied in grammar, to which we do not usually attend, and which do not even become obvious until you begin to compare languages. One of the most striking examples comes from Sapir (in Mandelbaum, 1958, pp. 157–159), and is well worth quoting in full. In reading it, bear in mind Vygotsky's example of expressing in words the single fact of a barefoot boy in a blue shirt running down the street.

> The natural or, at any rate, the naïve thing is to assume that when we wish to communicate a certain idea or impression, we make something like a rough and rapid inventory of the objective elements and relations involved in it, that such an inventory or analysis is quite inevitable, and that our linguistic task consists merely of the finding of the particular words and groupings of words that correspond to the terms of the objective analysis. Thus, when we observe an object of the type that we call a "stone" moving through space towards the earth, we involuntarily analyze the phenomenon into two concrete notions, that of a stone and that of an act of falling, and, relating these two notions to each other by certain formal methods proper to English, we declare that "the stone falls." We assume, naïvely enough, that this is about the only analysis that can properly be made. And yet, if we look into the ways that other languages take to express this very simple kind of impression, we soon realize how much may be added to,

subtracted from, or rearranged in our own form of expression without materially altering our report of the physical fact.

In German and in French we are compelled to assign "stone" to a gender category—perhaps the Freudians can tell us why this object is masculine in the one language, feminine in the other; in Chippewa we cannot express ourselves without bringing in the apparently irrelevant fact that a stone is an inanimate object. If we find gender beside the point, the Russians may wonder why we consider it necessary to specify in every case whether a stone, or any other object for that matter, is conceived in a definite or an indefinite manner, why the difference between "the stone" and "a stone" matters. "Stone falls" is good enough for Lenin, as it was good enough for Cicero. And if we find barbarous the neglect of the distinction as to definiteness, the Kwakiutl Indian of British Columbia may sympathize with us but wonder why we do not go a step further and indicate in some way whether the stone is visible or invisible to the speaker at the moment of speaking and whether it is nearest to the speaker, the person addressed, or some third party. "That would no doubt sound fine in Kwakiutl, but we are too busy!" And yet we insist on expressing the singularity of the falling object, where the Kwakiutl Indian, differing from the Chippewa, can generalize and make a statement which would apply equally well to one or several stones. Moreover, he need not specify the time of the fall. The Chinese get on with a minimum of explicit formal statement and content themselves with a frugal "stone fall."

These differences of analysis, one may object, are merely formal; they do not invalidate the necessity of the fundamental concrete analysis of the situation into "stone" and what the stone does, which in this case is "fall." But this necessity, which we feel so strongly, is an illusion. In the Nootka language the combined impression of a stone falling is quite differently analyzed. The stone need not be specifically referred to, but a single word, a verb form, may be used which is in practice not essentially more ambiguous than our English sentence. This verb form consists of two main elements, the first indicating general movement or position of a stone or stonelike object, while the second refers to downward direction. We can get some hint of the feeling of the Nootka word if we assume the existence of an intransitive verb "to stone," referring to the position or movement of a stonelike object. Then our sentence, "The stone falls," may be reassembled into something like "it stones down." In this type of expression the thing-quality of the stone is implied in the generalized verbal element "to stone," while the specific kind of motion which is given us in experience when a stone falls is conceived as separable into a generalized notion of the movement of a class of objects and a more specific one of direction. In other words, while Nootka has no difficulty whatever in describing the fall of a stone, it has no verb that truly corresponds to our "fall."

Examples such as these make it dramatically clear why the notion has been advanced that the grammatical categories of language *covertly* bring us to pay attention to different attributes of situations. Vygotsky may indeed have seen a barefoot boy in a blue shirt running down the street, but, as you have just seen, the translation from such a sense impression into a linguistic expression is no simple matter. Did this translation in any way affect what Vygotsky actually saw, or to what he was particularly sensitive in that event? This is an exceedingly difficult question to answer. Though direct evidence is lacking, one cannot help but feel that such obligatory grammatical distinctions as those discussed by Sapir do sensitize speakers to certain aspects of the world — at least when speaking.

To me a most graphic example of this suggestion is revealed by the use of pronouns of address in various languages (see Brown, 1965, Chapter 2). Take German, for example, where one must choose between the "familiar" *du* and the "polite" *Sie*, or between the corresponding *tu* and *vous* of French, using, at the same time, the appropriate verb conjugational forms. These are *obligatory* grammatical distinctions: when speaking German or French you must — whenever you talk to anyone — take note of what your relationship is to him in terms of status and intimacy, as defined by the norms of the society. Of course, even in English you often have to think of such things — you have to decide what style of speech to use, what topics to discuss, whether to use first name or title and last name, and so on. But I think that in comparing English with French or German, for example, we have a clear demonstration of the importance of an *obligatory* grammatical distinction in predisposing speakers to attend to certain things. Very often in English we can get away from these problems of social relations by just saying "you," talking generally, and never using a name. But, even more importantly, there are many situations in English when you simply never think much about the status and solidarity relations between yourself and the person to whom you are speaking. Think of the various people to whom you talk during a day — people you casually know in a course or at work, people you meet in the coffee room, people of various ages and status levels — I'm sure that most often you do not have to go through the sort of agonizing decision you would have to make in many cases if we were all compelled to speak French, for example, and thus were *constantly required* to decide which pronoun, or which verb form to use—in almost every remark. If we suddenly all switched to French, we would find our attention focussed on many aspects of social relations which were previously not of central concern. It is not that we never have to think of these things when speaking English, but that in speaking French, or some other language, we would almost certainly have to pay more daily attention to such matters.

Another sort of argument advanced on the grammatical front of the Whorf hypothesis is the matter of the part of speech membership of a word, and the semantic implications of such membership. For example, *heat*, in Indo-European languages, is a noun. A large number of nouns designate concrete things. Perhaps this is why so much fruitless effort was expended in the history of Western science in the search for a heat substance, like "phlogiston" and "caloric." Perhaps if Western scientists had spoken a language like Hopi, where *heat* is a verb, they may have started out with the more appropriate kinetic theory of heat at which they finally arrived. (But note that in spite of the language—if it *was* a determiner—Western scientists did eventually free themselves from the notion of a heat substance when this notion proved itself inadequate on empirical and rational grounds.)[1]

These numerous examples should give you a good idea of just how strikingly different languages can seem—different enough to have lead many thinkers to conclude that there must be some sort of cognitive relativity to correspond to the linguistic relativity. We could go on and on listing differences such as these—but the main point is simply that languages do seem rather different, one from the other, in the categories which they embody—both lexically and grammatically. If you look at all of these linguistic differences carefully, though, I think you will have to conclude that the striking differences between languages are not so much in what they are *able* to express, but in what they habitually do express and are required to express. Probably the basic *dimensions* along which linguistically-expressed categories vary are universals of human cognition. And probably the same basic *functions* are performed by all languages—making and negating assertions, asking questions, giving commands, and so on. Certainly the basic *form* of human language is universal. The strong form of the Whorfian hypothesis is appealing, but seductive (Whorf, 1956):

---

[1] In a similar vein, consider the many nouns used by psychologists—"mind," "behavior," "cognition," "rule," and the many more you have encountered in this book and elsewhere. Our vocabulary can lead us astray here as well, promoting an endless search for psychological or physiological "entities" where we ought to seek understanding of processes and dynamics, equilibrium and disequilibrium, and other more "verb-like" notions.

We cut nature up, organize it into concepts, and ascribe significances as we do, largely because we are parties to an agreement to organize it in this way—an agreement that holds throughout our speech community and is codified in the patterns of our language. The agreement is, of course, an implicit and unstated one, but its terms are absolutely obligatory; we cannot talk at all except by subscribing to the organization and classification of data which the agreement decrees.

If the statement were true in the bold form, certainly deaf children could not develop in the normal fashion revealed by Furth, as discussed above; and certainly linguistic science could not have achieved the striking successes it has achieved in describing features common to all human languages. A more modest, but also more acceptable formulation is offered by the linguist Charles Hockett (1954, p. 122):

Languages differ not so much as to what *can* be said in them, but rather as to what it is *relatively easy* to say in them. The history of Western logic and science constitutes not so much the story of scholars hemmed in and misled by the nature of their specific languages, as the story of a long and fairly successful struggle *against* inherited linguistic limitations. Where everyday language would not serve, special subsystems (mathematics, etc.) were devised. However, even Aristotle's development of syllogistic notation carries within itself aspects of Greek language structure.

The impact of an inherited linguistic pattern on activities is, in general, *least* important in the most practical contexts and most important in such "purely verbal" goings-on as storytelling, religion, and philosophizing. As a result, some types of literature are extremely difficult to translate accurately, let alone appealingly.

So much for abstract reasoning and anecdotal examples. The issues of linguistic relativity and determinism have been extremely difficult to study by the controlled methods of scientific psychology, but let us, finally, examine at least one concrete experiment which has been performed in an attempt to relate a specific aspect of a given language to a specific sort of behavior. From the point of view of the grand sweep of the Whorf hypothesis, such a restricted experiment may seem disappointing, but the problems of studying global relationships between a linguistic system and an entire world-view are obviously beyond our grasp.

An important collection of experiments was carried out in the late fifties in connection with the Southwest Project in Comparative Psycholinguistics (Carroll and Casagrande, 1958). A particularly interesting experiment from this Project deals with grammatical determinism in Navaho (p. 27):

> It is obligatory in the Navaho language, when using verbs of *handling*, to employ a particular one of a set of verbal forms according to the shape or some other essential attribute of the object about which one is speaking. Thus, if I ask you in Navaho to hand me an object, I must use the appropriate verb stem depending on the nature of the object. If it is a long flexible object such as a piece of string, I must say *šanléh*; if it is a long rigid object such as a stick, I must say *šańtįįh*; if it is a flat flexible material such as paper or cloth, I must say *šaniicóós*, and so on.

On the basis of this interesting grammatical distinction, Carroll and Casagrande proposed that (p. 27):

> Navaho-speaking children would learn to discriminate the "form" attributes of objects at an earlier age than their English-speaking compeers. The finding of American and European psychologists that children tend first to distinguish objects on the basis of size and color might—at least at the level of verbal facility in dealing with these variables—be partly an artifact of the particular language they use. The hypothesis was, then, that this feature of the Navaho language would affect the relative potency or order of emergence of such concepts as color, size, shape or form, and number in the Navaho-speaking child, as compared with English-speaking Navaho children of the same age, and that Navaho-speaking children would be more inclined than the latter to perceive formal similarities between objects.

The method was an object triads test, in which the child had to pick which two objects, of three presented, "went best" together. "For example, one of the pairs consisted of a yellow stick and a piece of blue rope of comparable size. The child was then shown a yellow rope, and the basis of his choice could be either color or the Navaho verb-form classification—since different verbal forms are used for a length of rope and a stick." Children were presented with triads such as blue rope—yellow rope—blue stick; small blue cube—medium blue cube—small blue sphere; blue stick—yellow stick—blue oblong block; and so on.
The experiment showed that: "In both the Navaho groups [Navaho-dominant and English-dominant children] . . . the trend is toward the increasing perceptual saliency of shape or form, as compared with color,

with increasing age. The curve starts lower and remains lower for English-dominant Navaho children, although it rises rather rapidly after the age of seven. Navaho children stay ahead of their English-speaking age mates, although the two curves tend to converge as age increases." In other words, children who speak only Navaho group on the basis of form or shape at an earlier age than those who speak English, although all of the children come from the same reservation, and live under similar circumstances. It thus appears that language has some effect on cognitive development in this case.

The picture becomes more complicated, however, when English-speaking children off the reservation are given the same test. Here we find a very interesting phenomenon. White American children in a Boston suburb are more similar to the Navaho-dominant than to the English-dominant Indians; that is, they tend early to sort on the basis of form and shape, rather than color. On the other hand, Black slum children in Harlem are more similar to the English-dominant Indians, giving up color matching at a later age. Thus two sorts of variables must be considered: environmental characteristics and native language. Carroll and Casagrande speculate that certain aspects of the environment of the white suburban child—perhaps playing with puzzles and toys which emphasize attention to form in themselves—can bring an English-speaking child to attend to form and shape at an early age. In an environment presumably lacking such nonlinguistic means of drawing attention to form (Indian reservations and urban slums), speaking a language like Navaho can accelerate cognitive development in regard to form versus color matching. As Carroll and Casagrande put it (p. 31):

> . . . we may amend our hypothesis in possibly the following form: The tendency of a child to match objects on the basis of form or material rather than size or color increases with age and may be enhanced by either of two kinds of experiences: (a) learning to speak a language like Navaho, which because of the central role played by form and material in its grammatical structure, requires the learner to make certain discriminations of form and material in the earlier stages of language learning in order to make himself understood at all; or (b) practice with toys and other objects involving the fitting of forms and shapes, and the resultant greater reinforcement received from form-matching.

One is reminded of Furth's discussion of the cognitive development of deaf children: language is but one of various ways of bringing a child to attend to certain attributes of the stimulus world.

The fate of the Sapir-Whorf hypothesis at the present time is interesting: today we are more concerned with linguistic universals and cultural universals than with linguistic and cultural relativity. Chomsky has suggested that Whorf was too much concerned with surface structures of languages, while on their deeper levels all languages are of the same universally human character. Cultural anthropologists are looking for ways in which the underlying structures of cultures are alike, and psychologists are moving out of Western culture to cross-cultural studies, in an attempt to understand general laws of human behavior and development. Perhaps in an age when our world has become so small, and the most diverse cultures so intimately interrelated in matters of war and peace, it is best that we come to an understanding of what all men have in common. But at the same time it would be dangerous to forget that different languages and cultures may indeed have important effects on what men will believe and what they will do.

Bibliography

Allport, G. W., & Postman, L. *The psychology of rumor.* New York: Russell & Russell Publishers, 1947.

Amster, H. Semantic satiation and generalization: learning? adaptation? *Psychological Bulletin*, 1964, 62, 273–286.

Bartlett, F. C. *Remembering: A study in experimental and social psychology.* Cambridge: Cambridge University Press, 1932.

Bellugi, U. The acquisition of negation. Unpublished doctoral dissertation, Harvard University, 1967.

Bellugi-Klima, U. Linguistic mechanisms underlying child speech. In E. M. Zale (Ed.), *Proceedings of the conference on language and language behavior.* New York: Appleton-Century-Crofts, 1968.

Berko, J. The child's learning of English morphology. *Word*, 1958, *14*, 150–177. [Also in S. Saporta (Ed.), *Psycholinguistics: A book of readings.* New York: Holt, Rinehart & Winston, 1961. Pp. 359–375.]

Bernstein, B. A socio-linguistic approach to socialisation: With some reference to educability. In J. J. Gumperz & D. Hymes (Eds.), *Directions in sociolinguistics.* New York: Holt, Rinehart & Winston, Inc., in press.

Black, M. (Ed.) *The importance of language.* Englewood Cliffs, N.J.: Prentice-Hall, Inc., 1962.

Bloom, L. M. Language development: Form and function in emerging grammars. Unpublished doctoral dissertation, Columbia University, 1968. [Cambridge, Mass.: M.I.T. Press, in press.]

Blount, B. G. Acquisition of language by Luo children. Unpublished doctoral dissertation, University of California, Berkeley, 1969.

Blumenthal, A. L. Prompted recall of sentences. *Journal of Verbal Learning and Verbal Behavior*, 1967, *6*, 203–206.

Blumenthal, A. L., & Boakes, R. Prompted recall of sentences. *Journal of Verbal Learning and Verbal Behavior*, 1967, *6*, 674–676.

Bowerman, M. F. Dissertation in preparation on acquisition of Finnish, Harvard University.

Braine, M. D. S. The ontogeny of English phrase structure: The first phase. *Language*, 1963, *39*, 1–13. [Also in R. D. Anderson & D. P.

Ausubel (Eds.), *Readings in the psychology of cognition.* New York: Holt, Rinehart & Winston, Inc., 1965. Pp. 303–320.]

Braine, M. D. S. The acquisition of language in infant and child. In C. Reed (Ed.), *The learning of language.* In press.

Brown, R. *Words and things.* Glencoe, III.: The Free Press, 1958.

Brown, R. *Psycholinguistics.* New York: The Free Press, 1965.

Brown, R. *Social psychology.* New York: The Free Press, 1970.

Brown, R., & Bellugi, U. Three processes in the child's acquisition of syntax. *Harvard educational Review,* 1964, *34,* 133–151. [Also in E. H. Lenneberg (Ed.), *New directions in the study of language.* Cambridge, Mass.: M.I.T. Press, 1964. Pp. 131–162.] [Also in R. Brown, *Psycholinguistics.* New York: The Free Press, 1970. Pp. 75–99.]

Brown, R., Cazden, C. B., & Bellugi, U. The child's grammar from I to III. Paper read at 1967 Minnesota Symposium on Child Psychology. Minneapolis, 1967.

Brown, R., Cazden, C. B., & Bellugi, U. The child's grammar from I to III. In J. P. Hill (Ed.), *Minnesota Symposia on Child Psychology,* Volume 2. Minneapolis: University of Minnesota Press, 1969. Pp. 28–73. [Also in R. Brown, *Psycholinguistics.* New York: The Free Press, 1970. Pp. 100–154.]

Brown, R., & Fraser, C. The acquisition of syntax. In C. N. Cofer & B. S. Musgrave (Eds.), *Verbal behavior and learning: Problems and processes.* New York: McGraw-Hill Book Company, 1963. Pp. 158–197. [Also in U. Bellugi & R. Brown (Eds.), The acquisition of language. *Monographs of the Society for Research in Child Development,* 1964, *29* (1), 43–79.]

Bruner, J. S., Olver, R. R., Greenfield, P. M., et al. *Studies in cognitive growth.* New York: John Wiley & Sons, Inc., 1966.

Carmichael, L., Hogan, H. P., & Walter, A. A. An experimental study of the effect of language on the representation of visually perceived form. *Journal of Experimental Psychology,* 1932, *15,* 73–86.

Carroll, J. B., & Casagrande, J. B. The function of language classification. In E. E. Maccoby et al. (Eds.), *Readings in social psychology* (3rd ed.). New York: Holt, Rinehart & Winston, Inc., 1958. Pp. 18–31.

Cazden, C. B. The acquisition of noun and verb inflections. *Child Development,* 1968, *39,* 433–448.

Chomsky, N. *Syntactic structures.* The Hague: Mouton, 1957.

Chomsky, N. A review of *Verbal behavior,* by B. F. Skinner. *Language,* 1959, *35,* 26–58. [Also in J. A. Fodor & J. J. Katz (Eds.), *The structure of language: Readings in the philosophy of language.* Englewood Cliffs, N.J.: Prentice-Hall, Inc., 1964. Pp. 547–578.] [Also in L. A. Jakobovits & M. S. Miron (Eds.), *Readings in the psychology of language.* Englewood Cliffs, N.J.: Prentice-Hall, Inc., 1967. Pp. 142–171.]

Chomsky, N. *Current issues in linguistic theory.* The Hague: Mouton, 1964. [Also in J. A. Fodor & J. J. Katz (Eds.), *The structure of lan-*

guage: Readings in the philosophy of language. Englewood Cliffs, N.J.: Prentice-Hall, Inc., 1964. Pp. 50–118.]

Chomsky, N. *Aspects of the theory of syntax.* Cambridge, Mass.: M.I.T. Press, 1965.

Chomsky, N. *Language and mind.* New York: Harcourt Brace Jovanovich, Inc., 1968.

Chomsky, N., & Halle, M. *The sound pattern of English.* New York: Harper & Row, Publishers, 1968.

Clark, H. H. Some structural properties of simple active and passive sentences. *Journal of Verbal Learning and Verbal Behavior*, 1965, *4*, 365–370.

Cofer, C. Experimental studies of the role of verbal processes in concept formation and problem solving. *Annals of the New York Academy of Science*, 1960, *91*, 94–107.

Cofer, C. N. (Ed.) *Verbal learning and verbal behavior.* New York: McGraw-Hill Book Company, 1961.

Cofer, C. N., & Musgrave, B. S. (Eds.) *Verbal behavior and learning: Problems and processes.* New York: McGraw-Hill Book Company, 1963.

Deese, J. On the structure of associative meaning. *Psychological Review*, 1962, *69*, 161–175.

Deese, J. The associative structure of some common English adjectives. *Journal of Verbal Learning and Verbal Behavior*, 1964, *3*, 347–357.

Deese, J. *The structure of associations in language and thought.* Baltimore: Johns Hopkins Press, 1965.

Eifermann, R. R. Negation: A linguistic variable. *Acta psychologica*, 1961, *18*, 258–273.

Ervin, S. M. Imitation and structural change in children's language. In E. H. Lenneberg (Ed.), *New directions in the study of language.* Cambridge, Mass.: M.I.T. Press, 1964. Pp. 163–189.

Ervin-Tripp, S. Language development. In M. Hoffman & L. Hoffman (Eds.), *Review of child development research.* Vol. 2. Ann Arbor: University of Michigan Press, 1966. Pp. 55–105.

Ervin-Tripp, S. M. & Slobin, D. I. Psycholinguistics. *Annual Review of Psychology*, 1966, *17*, 435–474.

Feather, B. W. Semantic generalization of classically conditioned responses: A review. *Psyohological Bulletin*, 1965, *63*, 425–441.

Ferguson, C. A., & Slobin, D. I. (Eds.) *Readings on child language acquisition.* New York: Holt, Rinehart & Winston, Inc., in press.

Fillmore, C. J. The case for case. In E. Bach & R. T. Harms (Eds.), *Universals in linguistic theory.* New York: Holt, Rinehart & Winston, Inc., 1968.

Fishman, J. A. A systematization of the Whorfian hypothesis. *Behavioral Science*, 1960, *5*, 1–29.

Fodor, J. A. Could meaning be an r_m? *Journal of Verbal Learning and Verbal Behavior*, 1965, *4*, 73–81. [Also in R. C. Oldfield & J. C.

Marshal (Eds.), *Language: Selected readings*. Baltimore: Penguin Books, Inc., 1968. Pp. 231–245.]

Fodor, J. A., & Bever, T. The psychological reality of linguistic segments. *Journal of Verbal Learning and Verbal Behavior,* 1965, *4*, 414–420. [Also in L. A. Jakobovits & M. S. Miron (Eds.), *Readings in the psychology of language.* Englewood Cliffs, N.J.: Prentice-Hall, Inc., 1964. Pp. 325–332.]

Fodor, J. A., & Katz, J. J. (Eds.) *The structure of language: Readings in the philosophy of language.* Englewood Cliffs, N.J.: Prentice-Hall, Inc., 1964.

Furth, H. G. Research with the deaf: Implications for language and cognition. *Psychological Bulletin*, 1964, *62*, 145–164.

Furth, H. G. *Thinking without language: Psychological implications of deafness.* New York: The Free Press, 1966.

Galton, F. Psychometric experiments. *Brain*, 1879, *2*, 149–162.

Garrett, M., Bever, T., & Fodor, J. A. The active use of grammar in speech perception. *Perception & Psychophysics,* 1966, *1*, 30–32.

Ghiselin, B. *The creative process.* New York: Mentor Books, 1955.

Gladwin, T., & Sturtevant, W. C. (Eds.) *Anthropology and human behavior.* Washington, D.C.: Anthropological Society of Washington, 1962.

Glanzer, M., & Clark, W. H. The verbal-loop hypothesis: Conventional figures. *American Journal of Psychology*, 1964, *77*, 621–626.

Gleason, H. A., Jr. *An introduction to descriptive linguistics* (Rev. Ed.). New York: Holt, Rinehart & Winston, Inc., 1961.

Gough, P. B. Grammatical transformations and speed of understanding. *Journal of Verbal Learning and Verbal Behavior*, 1965, *4*, 107–111.

Gough, P. B. The verification of sentences: The effects of delay of evidence and sentence length. *Journal of Verbal Learning and Verbal Behavior,* 1966, *5,* 492–496.

Gumperz, J. J., & Hymes, D. (Eds.) *Directions in socio-linguistics.* New York: Holt, Rinehart & Winston, Inc., in press.

Hayhurst, H. Some errors of young children in producing passive sentences. *Journal of Verbal Learning and Verbal Behavior,* 1967, *6*, 654–660.

Herman, D. T., Lawless, R. H., & Marshall, R. W. Variables in the effect of language on the reproduction of visually perceived forms. *Perceptual & Motor Skills,* 1957, *7*, Monograph Supplement 2, 171–186. [Also in S. Saporta (Ed.), *Psycholinguistics: A book of readings.* New York: Holt, Rinehart & Winston, Inc., 1961. Pp. 537–551.]

Hockett, C. F. Chinese vs. English: An exploration of the Whorfian thesis. In H. Hoijer (Ed.), *Language in culture.* Chicago: The University of Chicago Press, 1954.

Hymes, D. H. (Ed.) *Language in culture and society: A reader in linguistics and anthropology.* New York: Harper & Row, Publishers, 1964.

Inhelder, B., Bovet, M., Sinclair, H., & Smock, C. D. On cognitive development. *American Psychologist,* 1966, *21*, 160–164.

Jacobs, R. A., & Rosenbaum, P. S. *English transformational grammar.* Waltham, Mass.: Blaisdell Publishing Co., 1968.

Jakobson, R. *Child language, aphasia, and phonological universals.* The Hague: Mouton, 1968. [Translation of *Kindersprache, Aphasie und allgemeine Lautgesetze.* Uppsala: Almqvist & Wiksell, 1941.]

Jakobson, R., & Halle, M. *Fundamentals of language.* The Hague: Mouton, 1956.

James, W. *Psychology: Briefer course.* New York: Henry Holt & Co., 1892.

Jenkins, J. J., & Palermo, D. S. Mediation processes and the acquisition of linguistic structure. In U. Bellugi & R. Brown (Eds.), *The acquisition of Language. Monographs of the Society for Research in Child Development,* 1964, *29* (1), 141–169.

Jespersen, O. *The philosophy of grammar.* London: Holt, Rinehart & Winston, Inc., 1924.

Katz, J. J., & Fodor, J. A. The structure of a semantic theory. *Language,* 1963, *39*, 170–210. [Also in J. A. Fodor & J. J. Katz (Eds.), *The structure of language: Readings in the philosophy of language.* Englewood Cliffs, N.J.: Prentice-Hall, Inc., 1964. Pp. 479–518.]

Katz, J. J., & Postal, P. M. *An integrated theory of linguistic descriptions.* Cambridge, Mass.: M.I.T. Press, 1964.

Kent, G. H., & Rosanoff, A. J. A study of association in insanity. *American Journal of Insanity,* 1910, *67*, 317–390.

Kernan, K. T. The acquisition of language by Samoan children. Unpublished doctoral dissertation, University of California, Berkeley, 1969.

Klima, E. S., & Bellugi, U. Syntactic regularities in the speech of children. In J. Lyons & R. J. Wales (Eds.), *Psycholinguistics papers: The proceedings of the 1966 Edinburgh conference.* Edinburgh: Edinburgh University Press, 1966. Pp. 183–208.

Kohlberg, L., Yaeger, J., & Hjertholm, E. Private speech: Four studies and a review of theories. *Child Development,* 1968, *39*, 691–736.

Lantz, D. L. & Stefflre, V. Language and cognition revisited. *Journal of Abnormal and Social Psychology,* 1964, *69*, 472–481.

Lashley, K. S. The problem of serial order in behavior. In L. A. Jeffress (Ed.), *Cerebral mechanisms in behavior.* New York: John Wiley & Sons, Inc., 1951. Pp. 112–136. [Also in S. Saporta (Ed.), *Psycholinguistics: A book of readings.* New York: Holt, Rinehart & Winston, Inc., 1961. Pp. 180–198.]

Lees, R. B. A review of N. Chomsky's *Syntactic structures. Language,* 1957, *33*, 375–408.

Lenneberg, E. H. Understanding language without ability to speak: A case report. *Journal of Abnormal and Social Psychology,* 1962, *65*, 419–425.

Lenneberg, E. H. *Biological foundations of language.* New York: John Wiley & Sons, Inc., 1967.

Liberman, A. M., Cooper, F. S., Shankweiler, D. P., & Studdert-Kennedy, M. Perception of the speech code. *Psychological Review,* 1967, *74,* 431–461.

Luria A. R. Razvitiye rechi v formirovaniye psikhicheskikh protzessov [Speech development in the formation of mental processes]. In *Psikhologicheskaya nauka v SSSR.* Vol. I. Moscow: Akad. Pedag. Nauk RSFSR, 1959. Pp. 516–577. [Translation in *Psychological science in the USSR.* Vol. I. Washington, D.C.: U.S. Joint Publ. Res. Serv. No. 11466, 1961. Pp. 704–787.]

Luria, A. R., & Vinogradova, O. S. An objective investigation of the dynamics of semantic systems. *British Journal of Psychology,* 1959, *50,* 89–105.

Lyons, J., & Wales, R. J. (Eds.) *Psycholinguistics papers: The proceedings of the 1966 Edinburgh conference.* Edinburgh: Edinburgh University Press, 1966.

Mandelbaum, D. B. (Ed.) *Selected writings of Edward Sapir in language, culture and personality.* Berkeley and Los Angeles: University of California Press, 1958.

McCawley, J. D. The role of semantics in a grammar. In E. Bach & R. T. Harms (Eds.), *Universals in linguistic theory.* New York: Holt, Rinehart & Winston, Inc., 1968. Pp. 125–170.

McMahon, L. E. Grammatical analysis as part of understanding a sentence. Unpublished doctoral dissertation, Harvard University, 1963.

McNeill, D. Developmental psycholinguistics. In F. Smith & G. A. Miller (Eds.), *The genesis of language: A psycholinguistic approach.* Cambridge, Mass.: M.I.T. Press, 1966. Pp. 15–84.

McNeill, D. The development of language. In P. H. Mussen (Ed.), *Carmichael's manual of child psychology.* 3rd ed. Vol. 1. New York: John Wiley & Sons, Inc., 1970. Pp. 1061–1161.

Mehler, J. Some effects of grammatical transformations on the recall of English sentences. *Journal of Verbal Learning and Verbal Behavior,* 1963, *2,* 346–351.

Miller, G. A. *Language and communication.* New York: McGraw-Hill Book Company, 1951.

Miller, G. A. The magical number seven, plus or minus two: Some limits on our capacity for processing information. *Psychological Review,* 1956, *63,* 81–97.

Miller, G. A. Some psychological studies of grammar. *American Psychologist,* 1962, *17,* 748–762. [Also in L. A. Jakobovits & M. S. Miron (Eds.), *Readings in the psychology of language.* Englewood Cliffs, N.J.: Prentice-Hall, Inc., 1967. Pp. 201–218.

Miller, G. A., & Chomsky, N. Finitary models of language users. In R. D. Luce, R. R. Bush, & E. Galanter (Eds.), *Handbook of mathematical psychology.* Vol. 2. New York: John Wiley & Sons, Inc., 1963. Pp. 419–491.

Miller, G. A., Galanter, E., & Pribram, K. *Plans and the structure of behavior.* New York: Holt, Rinehart & Winston, Inc., 1960.

Miller, G. A., & Isard, S. Free recall of self-embedded English sentences. *Information & Control*, 1964, 7, 292–303.

Miller, G. A., & McKean, K. O. A chronometric study of some relations between sentences. *Quarterly Journal of Experimental Psychology*, 1964, *16*, 297–308. [Also in R. C. Oldfield & J. C. Marshall (Eds.), *Language: Selected Readings.* Baltimore: Penguin Books, Inc., 1968. Pp. 213–230.]

Miller, G. A., & McNeill, D. Psycholinguistics. In G. Lindzey & E. Aronson (Eds.), *The handbook of social psychology* (2nd ed.). Vol. 3. Reading, Mass.: Addison-Wesley Publishing Co., Inc., 1969. Pp. 666–794.

Miller, W. R. The acquisition of formal features of language. *American Journal of Orthopsychiatry*, 1963, *34*, 862–867.

Miller, W. R., & Ervin, S. M. The development of grammar in child language. In U. Bellugi & R. Brown (Eds.), *The acquisition of language. Monographs of the Society for Research in Child Development*, 1964, *29* (1), 9–33.

Mowrer, O. H. *Learning theory and the symbolic process.* New York: John Wiley & Sons, Inc., 1960.

Nida, E. A. Analysis of meaning and dictionary making. *International Journal of American Linguistics*, 1958, *24*, 279–292.

Ogden, C. K., & Richards, I. A. *The meaning of meaning.* New York: Harcourt Brace Jovanovich, Inc., 1923.

Oldfield, R. C., & Marshall, J. C. (Eds.) *Language: Selected readings.* Baltimore: Penguin Books, Inc., 1968.

Osgood, C. E. The nature and measurement of meaning. *Psychological Bulletin*, 1952, *49*, 197–237.

Osgood, C. E. *Method and theory in experimental psychology.* New York: Oxford University Press, 1953. Part IV, pp. 601–727.

Osgood, C. E. Psycholinguistics. In S. Koch (Ed.), *Psychology: A study of a science.* Vol. 6. New York: McGraw-Hill Book Company, 1963. Pp. 244–316.

Osgood, C. E., Suci, G. J., & Tannenbaum, P. H. *The measurement of meaning.* Urbana: University of Illinois Press, 1957.

Penfield, W., & Roberts, L. *Speech and brain mechanisms.* Princeton, N.J.: Princeton University Press, 1959.

Piaget, J. *Le langage et la pensée chez l'enfant.* Neuchâtel and Paris: Delachaux & Niestle, 1923. [Translation: *The language and thought of the child.* New York: Meridan, 1955.]

Piaget, J. *The construction of reality in the child.* New York: Basic Books, Inc., Publishers, 1954.

Piaget, J. *Comments on Vygotsky's critical remarks concerning "The Language and Thought of the Child" and "Judgment and Reasoning in the Child."* Cambridge, Mass.: M.I.T. Press, 1962. (a)

Piaget, J. *Play, dreams and imitation in childhood.* New York: W. W. Norton & Company, Inc., 1962. (b)

Postal, P. M. Underlying and superficial linguistic structure. *Harvard Educational Review*, 1964, *34*, 246–266. [Also in R. C. Oldfield & J. C. Marshall (Eds.), *Language: Selected readings*. Baltimore: Penguin Books, Inc., 1968. Pp. 179–201.]

Rohrman, N. L. The role of syntactic structure in the recall of English nominalizations. *Journal of Verbal Learning and Verbal Behavior*, 1968, *7*, 904–912.

Romney, A. K., & D'Andrade, R. G. Cognitive aspects of English kin terms. In A. K. Romney & R. G. D'Andrade (Eds.), *Transcultural studies in cognition. American Anthropologist*, 1964, *66* (No. 3, Part 2), 146–170.

Romney, A. K. & D'Andrade, R. G. (Eds.) *Transcultural studies in cognition. American Anthropologist,* 1964, *66* (No. 3, Part 2).

Sachs, J. S. Recognition memory for syntactic and semantic aspects of connected discourse. *Perception & Psychophysics,* 1967, *2,* 437–442.

Sapir, E. Language and environment. *American Anthropologist*, 1912, n.s., 226–242. [Also in D. G. Mandelbaum (Ed.), *Selected writings of Edward Sapir in language, culture and personality*. Berkeley and Los Angeles: University of California Press, 1958. Pp. 89–103.]

Saporta, S. (Ed.) *Psycholinguistics: A book of readings.* New York: Holt, Rinehart & Winston, Inc., 1961.

Sartre, J.-P. *Nausea.* New York: New Directions Pub. Corp., 1959.

Savin, H. B., & Perchonock, E. Grammatical structure and the immediate recall of English sentences. *Journal of Verbal Learning and Verbal Behavior*, 1965, *4*, 348–353.

Schachtel, E. G. *Metamorphosis.* New York: Basic Books, Inc., Publishers, 1959. (Chap. 12: "On memory and childhood amnesia.")

Searle, J. R. *Speech acts: An essay in the philosophy of language.* Cambridge: Cambridge University Press, 1969.

Sechenov, I. M. Refleksy golovnogo mozga [Reflexes of the brain]. *Meditzinskiy vestnik,* 1863, *3*, 461–464, 493–512.

Shvartz, L. A. Uslovnyye refleksy na slovenyye razdrazhiteli [conditioned responses to verbal stimuli]. *Voprosy psikhologii,* 1960, *6* (1), 86–98.

Skinner, B. F. *Verbal behavior.* New York: Appleton-Century-Crofts, 1957.

Slobin, D. I. Grammatical transformations in childhood and adulthood. Unpublished doctoral dissertation, Harvard University, 1963.

Slobin, D. I. Grammatical transformations in childhood and adulthood. *Journal of Verbal Learning and Verbal Behavior*, 1966, *5*, 219–227. (a)

Slobin, D. I. Soviet psycholinguistics. In N. O'Connor (Ed.), *Present-day Russian psychology: A symposium by seven authors*. Oxford: Pergamon Press, 1966. Pp. 109–151. (b)

Slobin, D. I. (Ed.) *A field manual for cross-cultural study of the acqui-*

sition of communicative competence. Berkeley: University of California, ASUC Bookstore, 1967.

Slobin, D. I. Recall of full and truncated passive sentences in connected discourse. *Journal of Verbal Learning and Verbal Behavior*, 1968, *7*, 876–881.

Slobin, D. I. Early grammatical development in several languages, with special attention to Soviet research. In W. Weksel and T. G. Bever (Eds.), *The structure and psychology of language.* New York: Holt, Rinehart & Winston, Inc., in press. (a)

Slobin, D. I. (Ed.) *The ontogenesis of grammar.* New York: Academic Press, Inc., in press. (b)

Slobin, D. I., & Welsh, C. A. Elicited imitation as a research tool in developmental psycholinguistics. In C. A. Ferguson & D. I. Slobin (Eds.), *Readings on child language acquisition.* New York: Holt, Rinehart & Winston, Inc., in press.

Smith, E. M., Brown, H. O., Toman, J. E. P., & Goodman, L. S. The lack of cerebral effects of *d*-tubocurarine. *Anesthesiology*, 1947, *8*, 1–14.

Spiker, C. C. Verbal factors in the discrimination learning of children. *Monographs of the Society for Research in Child Development*, 1963, *28* (2), 53–68.

Staats, A. W., & Staats, C. K. *Complex human behavior: A systematic extension of learning principles.* New York: Holt, Rinehart & Winston, Inc., 1963.

Turner, E. A., & Rommetveit, R. The acquisition of sentence voice and reversibility. *Child Development,* 1967, *38*, 649–660. (a)

Turner, E. A., & Rommetveit, R. Experimental manipulation of the production of active and passive voice in children. *Language and Speech*, 1967, *10*, 169–180. (b)

Turner, E. A., & Rommetveit, R. Focus of attention in recall of active and passive sentences. *Journal of Verbal Learning and Verbal Behavior*, 1968, *7*, 543–548.

Velten, H. V. The growth of phonemic and lexical patterns in infant language. *Language*, 1943, *19*, 281–292.

Vygotsky, L. S. *Thought and language.* Cambridge, Mass.: M.I.T. Press, 1962.

Wallace, A. F. C., & Atkins, J. The meaning of kinship terms. *American Anthropologist,* 1960, *62*, 58–79.

Wason, P. C. The processing of positive and negative information. *Quarterly Journal of Experimental Psychology,* 1959, *11*, 92–107.

Wason, P. C. Response to affirmative and negative binary statements. *British Journal of Psychology,* 1961, *52*, 133–142.

Wason, P. C. The contexts of plausible denial. *Journal of Verbal Learning and Verbal Behavior,* 1965, *4*, 7–11. [Also in R. C. Oldfield & J. C. Marshall (Eds.), *Language: Selected readings.* Baltimore: Penguin Books, Inc., 1968. Pp. 246–253.]

Watson, J. B. Psychology as the behaviorist views it. *Psychological Review*, 1913, *20*, 158–177.

Weksel, W., & Bever, T. G. (Eds.) *The structure and psychology of language.* New York: Holt, Rinehart & Winston, Inc., in press.

Whorf, B. L. *Language, thought, and reality.* (Edited with an introduction by J. B. Carroll.) Cambridge, Mass. and New York: M.I.T. Press and John Wiley & Sons, Inc., 1956.

Name Index

Subject Index

Ambiguity, 5–6, 11, 87, 88
Amnesia, childhood, 105–109
Anomaly, 2, 4, 86, 87, 88
Antonyms, 82–84
Association, 9, 56, 78–84, 89, 93n
Associative meaning, 79, 81
Auxiliary verb, 16–17

Behaviorism, 19, 40, 49–50, 88–93, 98
Box diagram, 13
Bracketing, 11, 13
Bulgarian, child language, 46n

Cognitive development, 56, 99, 109–120, 132
Competence, linguistic, 4, 6, 7–8, 19, 22, 37, 86, 87, 88
Complexity, linguistic, 23, 28, 29, 33–36
Componential analysis, 70–78
Comprehension: see understanding
Constituent structures: see phrase structure grammar
Context, 7, 33–37, 88, 94, 95, 112, 113
Critical stage for language acquisition, 56

Deaf children, 115–117, 130
Deep structure: see structure
Disambiguation, 6, 87, 98n
Discontinuous elements, 10, 18, 27
Distinctive features, phonological, 62–64, 69, 78

Egocentric speech, 117–119
Embedded sentences, 10, 14, 27

Finnish, child language, 46n
French, child language, 46n
Functions of speech, 46, 118–120

Generative grammar, 6, 13, 15–20, 56, 68
German, child language, 46n
Grammar, generative: see generative grammar
Grammar, phrase structure: see Phrase structure grammar
Grammar, transformational: see Transformational grammar
Grammatical relations, 5, 46n, 47, 48
Grammaticality, 4–5, 23, 54

Hesitation in child speech, 48
Hierarchical organization, 12, 25
development of, 47–48

Image theory of meaning, 91–92
Imitation, 19, 43, 49, 52, 59, 60, 64
Inflections, development of, 49–50, 53
Inner speech, 100, 101, 118, 119
Interrogation, 51

Japanese, child language, 46n

Kinship terms, 70–76

Learning theory, 56, 57, 60, 61, 93
Left-to-right model, 8–12, 14, 60
Linguistic relativity and determinism: see Whorfian hypothesis
Luo, child language, 46n